God's Mighty Dollar

Understanding God's
Financial Plan

By
Deborah C. Alexander, MBA

God's Mighty Dollar
by Deborah C. Alexander

Copyright ©2019 Deborah C. Alexander, All rights reserved

Published by
Partnership Publications, A Division of House To House Publications
Lititz, Pennsylvania 17543

ISBN-13: 978-1-7330137-0-3
ISBN-10: 1-7330137-0-9

Library of Congress Control Number: 2019941459

Scripture quotations taken from AMPLIFIED BIBLE, Copyright © 1954, 1958, 1962, 1964, 1965, 1987 by The Lockman Foundation. All rights reserved. Used by permission (www.Lockman.org).

Scripture taken from the Common English Bible ®, CEB ® Copyright © 2010, 2011 by Common English Bible ™. Used by permission. All rights reserved worldwide. The "CEB" and "Common English Bible" trademarks are registered in the United States Patent and Trademark Office by Common English Bible. Use of either trademark requires the permission of Common English Bible.

Scripture taken from the HOLY BIBLE, NEW INTERNATIONAL VERSION ®, Copyright © 1973, 1978, 1984 by International Bible Society, Used by permission of Zondervan. All rights reserved.

Scripture taken from the New King James Version, Copyright©1982 by Thomas Nelson, Inc. Used by permission. All rights reserved.

Scripture quotations marked NLT are taken from the Holy Bible, New Living Translation, copyright © 1996, 2004, 2015 by Tyndale House Foundation. Used by permission of Tyndale House Publishers, Inc., Carol Stream, Illinois 60188. All rights reserved.

Scripture quotations marked KJV are taken from the King James Version.

Disclaimer: This book is intended to provide biblical and practical information regarding the stated subject matter. The author and publisher are not providing professional, financial or legal advice and accept no liability from the use of items discussed in this book. Such services should be obtained by licensed professionals.

This book or parts thereof may not be reproduced in any form, without written permission of the author except as provided by the United States of America copyright law.

> "When someone you love says goodbye
> you can stare long and hard at the door
> they closed and forget to see all the
> doors God has open in front of you."
> – Shannon Alder

In Memoriam

In memoriam of my husband, Donald Alexander, Sr. and son, Devin C. Alexander, who went to be with the Lord.

Much of my spiritual growth can be attributed to Don's wisdom and sincere love for God that he openly displayed. He often counseled me and offered gentle guidance when I sought his opinion. Don always said that it was important to trust God above everything else. I have come to value this advice more and more as I journey through my new life without him. He has left an indelible mark. I will always cherish the thirty-seven years we spent together.

Devin was such a loving, jovial son. His gregarious nature made everyone his friend. He enjoyed life and wanted those he encountered to enjoy life with him. Though his unexpected departure from this life at the age of seventeen was difficult in many ways, the warm memories delight my heart. As I wrote, I thought about my "Debbie Card" (debit card) and how Devin knew there would always be money in the account for him. Thanks to God, I have learned how and when to use my "Debbie Card" wisely and I have found that God indeed does provide all my needs.

Foreword
By Bishop Silas Johnson

It has been said quite aptly, "Money makes a wonderful servant but a terrible master." Unfortunately far too many people, including believers, have not risen to the point of mastering their finances. The primary reason for this is they have never matured in, nor mastered, the principles that govern and guarantee financial prosperity.

In this insightful book, *God's Mighty Dollar, Understanding God's Financial Plan*, author Deborah Alexander lays out in a precise, practical, and provocative manner God's plan for financial freedom and abundance. From the Garden of Eden to the age of Wall Street, Debbie outlines and demonstrates for the reader line upon line, precept upon precept, God's ageless, venerable, time-tested laws of financial stewardship.

Although she holds a MBA, has years of corporate management experience, and a wealth of biblical knowledge, perhaps her most unique qualifying experience is the fact that Debbie is a widow. Throughout the Bible, from the widow woman of Zarephath to the widow Jesus observed casting her last two mites into the offering, widows understand perhaps above all others the most important element of biblical stewardship…trusting God.

I believe as you apply the profound teachings and wonderful anecdotes contained in this book you will truly learn to trust the Almighty with your money. Then you, like Debbie, will discover for yourself the power of *God's Mighty Dollar*.

Acknowledgments

First and foremost, I would like to thank my heavenly Father for breathing life into this work. Without Him, His vision, and plan for my life, I would not have been able to do this. Through this process, I have learned, and I am still learning how to trust, lean on and depend upon God for everything. While I do not profess to know all there is to know about money, I know Him, the creator of the earth and all that is within it. Thank you, Father, for giving me the desire to share all that You have shown me with others so that they, too, can experience the abundant life that exists in and through You.

Special thanks go to my son, Donald, Jr. and daughter-in-law, Tasha. I deeply appreciate the afternoons and evenings that you spent listening to me as I went through my initial thought processes. Having the approval of my children is invaluable and it confirms to me what a treasure both of you are.

My coach, counselor, mentor and nephew, Dr. Lawrence Bolar, has been there at every turn. Thank you, Lawrence, for motivating and pushing me forward, making me press toward the mark. Your wisdom as a published author and educator is much appreciated. Your time, insight and direction mean a lot to me. The love we share as family truly has been demonstrated through your actions.

My brother-in-law, Reverend Ray N. Smith, Sr. has been a guiding star for me. Ray, you listened, critiqued and gave much-needed feedback from your years in ministry. You invoked my thought processes to ensure that I was mindful of those who read this. I am grateful for your consistency and the holy example that you are to our family. You and Karlyn have always been there for me when I was a child and now as I branch out into this new territory. Your words of wisdom and faith are very much appreciated.

Dr. Jennifer Johnson, Executive Pastor and first lady of Full Counsel Metro Church, has been an encouragement to me through her prophetic voice. Thank you, Pastor Jennifer, for fearlessly speaking God's blessings over me and providing much appreciated feedback on this book. I know that your time is limited, yet you were willing to invest in me as I endeavored to embark upon this venture. You are an example not only for me but also for many others.

Last, but certainly not least, I acknowledge my friend, Edith Lambert, an educator and phenomenal teacher. Your soft-spoken words of wisdom are Spirit-filled and enlightening. Thank you so much for hearing and reading what I have to say. I especially appreciate your tireless reviews of each revision and the much needed feedback that you provided. I value our friendship and all that you have done for me. When you gave me the pen with the inscription "Write it down," you prophesied this book. Thank you for helping me to step into my future and widen my horizons.

CONTENTS

Introduction 11

Chapter 1: The Beginning – How It All Started 17

Chapter 2: God's Plan 27

Chapter 3: God is a God of Principles 39

Chapter 4: The Principles of Ownership
and Stewardship 51

Chapter 5: The Principle of the Tithe 61

Chapter 6: The Principles of Saving and Investing ... 81
Responsible Choices

Chapter 7: The Principles of Sowing and Reaping 95
The Law of Divine Reciprocity

Chapter 8: Displaced Trust 113

Chapter 9: Decision Time 121

Chapter 10: Stepping Into the Future 135

Introduction

Prophecy from Dr. Jennifer Johnson
The Prophetic Voice Ministry
November 12, 2017

> "Surely the Lord God will do nothing, but He revealeth his secret unto His servants the prophets." – Amos 3:7 (KJV)

"When you retire, Debbie, Ms. Debbie, God said that He has full time work for you in His house. 'You are going to be working, not obligated to set hours or anything like that, but your work, your finished work for the latter days is in My house.

'Everything that I have put in you, the knowledge and the skills, everything that I began, now you are going to reap and you are going to dedicate it to my house. When I meet you, I am going to say "well done, my good and faithful servant." You have finished the work. Not only have you finished the work that I placed in you, but you finished the work of and the legacy of Pastor Alexander.'

"The hand of God is upon you, and you will double because you are working not only by the strength of your hands but the strength of the Holy Spirit Himself. Those are tears of joy. You know that it's the word of God because I prophesied to you before and you told me that it was true. I saw you in your bedroom and you know that I was not in your house, but God showed me. 'Minister Debbie, I am raising you with an anointing of the work that I called you to, but Don's name shall carry on in this life because I, the Lord, will make sure that it's done. His work is going to be finished.'

"You are going to do this and it's going to be done with supernatural strength. You are not going to be tired or weary. The spirit of grief is going to be completely demolished off your life–-annihilated because you are going to be working so hard for God. He is going to send you a team that is going to help you. Now, believe that!"

The bird's eye view of my journey began on October 28, 2016, when I had a dream. I knew that this dream was different, and more than a figment of my imagination. I can remember it vividly, as I have remembered every other prophetic dream that I had in the past. I wrote it down because the Bible says to write the vision and make it plain. In my dream, I saw myself in my bed, lying diagonally. This showed me that it was no longer life as usual because I was not confined to a specific side of the bed. My head was on the side where my husband normally slept and my feet were on my side of the bed. I was venturing into a life that included a portion of him and me. When asked what I was doing, I said that I was having a baby remotely. Being that I am unmarried and my husband has gone to be with the Lord, I knew that the baby that I was to birth was symbolic of a new life and purpose to come directly from God. I had to wait for it to come to life.

In the meantime, I developed an insatiable hunger for the things of God. I read the Bible daily, often for hours. I listened to many sermons and read numerous books. I researched topics of interest to learn more. God heightened my knowledge and understanding of Him and His Word. I began to listen more closely for His voice in everything that I endeavored to do.

I received the prophetic word recorded above from Dr. Jennifer Johnson and held on to its veracity. It was confirmation of what God had given Dr. Jennifer in the past to speak to me. God had also given me signs of His plans through my friend Edith. Both Edith and Dr. Jennifer had told me that I was to write and that my writing would include workbooks. At that time, I did not know how all of this would materialize, as I was still working at a very demanding job and there was little leisure time. But…God has a way of changing things.

On April 17, 2018, I retired from my fulltime job. The company for which I worked had gone through multiple internal changes and I felt that I could not continue there and maintain the level of happiness and contentment that I wanted and needed. Therefore, I chose to leave and pursue other goals. As I began to review my life and objectives, it became clear that God had something for me to do. I did not know how it would work or what course of action I would take. There was heightened excitement and expectation of good things to come. Now, there would be sufficient time to work on the things that bring true fulfillment.

A few weeks after leaving my job, I felt a strong desire to go to my Bishop, Silas Johnson, and let Him know that I felt God telling me to work with the grief ministry that Bishop Johnson had envisioned. Bishop Johnson told me to develop my plans and present them to him. I gave him everything that God had shown me and approval was granted to implement the grief ministry. I solicited three diverse, Spirit-filled, professional women who had experienced the loss of their husbands to work with me and the Comfort Zone Grief Ministry was launched at our church. Our team has ministered to those who experience loss and grief with compassion and application of the Word of God. This ministry has been a blessing to me, the team members and those who seek our meetings as refuge in search of comfort and direction during the time of bereavement.

Many times women who have been left alone after the passing of their husbands experience financial hardships. I knew that they and many others in the church could benefit from the things I had learned through my personal journeys and how the application of God's principles helped me to navigate through many difficult times. I wrote this book to provide insight and hope to them and others.

I believe with all of my innermost being that God desires for us to prosper and that He has provided means for us to have and enjoy an abundant life, a life of peace and sufficiency. He has appropriated more than enough to meet and exceed our needs. Unfortunately, many of us have been deceived into thinking that we cannot, should not, and will not be prosperous. While all of us may not ever have a million dollars, we can have "good success," if we learn how to live and give using the principles that God has provided.

The dreams God gave me and the words of prophecy that have been spoken over me are truly coming to pass. God's word does not return to Him void. They surely accomplish the things that He sent them to do. I am more content now that I am walking in the purpose that God planned for me.

God's Mighty Dollar

CHAPTER 1

The Beginning —
How It All Started

> "You weren't an accident. You weren't mass produced. You aren't an assembly-line product. You were deliberately planned, specifically gifted, and lovingly positioned on the Earth by the Master Craftsman." – Max Lucado

"For I know the plans I have for you declares the Lord, plans to prosper you and not to harm you, plans to give you hope and a future" (Jeremiah 29:11, NIV).

From the beginning, God's plan was for man to prosper in every aspect of life, having control of everything that affects us mentally, physically and spiritually. God wants us to have an abundance or sufficiency to meet and/or exceed every need. Yet, most of us are not living the life that God planned for us to live. Jesus said "The thief does not come except to steal, and to kill, and to destroy. I have come that they may have life and that they may have it more abundantly" (John 10:10, NKJV). The abundant life is a life that is enriching and full in every aspect. Life to the fullness includes first and foremost an intimate relationship with God through Jesus Christ and the pursuit of God's plans for us. We are to contribute to God's kingdom and enjoy the provisions that He has set aside for us. God does not want us to suffer through life with our needs being unmet.

When the children of Israel left Egypt headed to the Promised Land, God gave them many promises of provision. Deuteronomy 28:8 says "The Lord will command the blessing on you in your storehouses and in all to which you set your hand, and He will bless you in the land which the Lord your God is giving you" (NKJV). In this scripture, we clearly see that God wants His people to be blessed and successful, having all sufficiency in all things. The one caveat seen in verse nine of that same chapter is that we would follow His commandments. Hence, to receive all that God has in store, we must live according to His will and obey His Word. But, just like Israel, many of us fall short of walking in the commanded blessings of God.

When asking many Christians and non-Christians alike how they are doing, the response is often "I'm going through." This term is indicative of one going through a test, trial, or tribulation that may result from various reasons. Sometimes, we create our own misery, and want others to take the blame or assume responsibility for a situation that was avoidable. We mishandle money, make poor decisions to buy things we cannot afford, using charge accounts and create bills we cannot pay.

Other times, we may encounter hardships caused by no fault of our own. A job lay-off that affects an entire company or a sickness resulting in exorbitant medical bills can negatively impact even the most fiscally responsible. Regardless of how one encounters the day of financial reckoning, it is a sobering moment. Only after realizing that money—actually the love of it and what it can acquire—is controlling us by stealing our peace, sleep, happiness and much more, do many people finally seek ways to change.

Instead of being the tool intended for life and the Kingdom of God, money has become an elusive seductress captivating hearts and minds – rich or poor, black or white, saved and unsaved. Consequently, the influencing power and biblical significance of money often takes a back seat to the tight clinches of fear, misuse or abuse. Acquisition and use of money often become a life goal, rather than the pursuit of God's divine purpose for life. Ecclesiastes 10:19 says: "A feast is made for laughter, and wine maketh merry: but money answereth all things" (KJV). Looking at this scripture on the surface, one may erroneously conclude that our major focus in life is to seek and acquire money. The scripture is not saying that we must seek money. Rather, we must use money as a tool and resource.

According to Strong's Exhaustive Concordance of the Bible, the word "answereth," as used in Ecclesiastes 10:19 means, among other things, to heed, to speak to, and bring low.[i] From this definition, we see the source of the saying "money talks." People listen to those who have money and give more attention to them. Money also makes things more accessible, opening doors to opportunities that may not be available to a person of limited resources.

As a member of the management team in a major corporation, I was responsible for my departmental budget. Each year, the divisional team would meet to determine how to allocate resources among the respective departments. Each manager would review his or her budget and justify the need for assistance from the Information Technology team. Requests that could be completed quickly were identified as low-hanging fruit. The low cost of the item made it an accessible opportunity and those projects were quickly approved. These requests were "answered" because the nominal investments brought immediate returns.

I know that many of you have gone to your favorite restaurant and asked to be seated in a certain server's area. The server had waited on you in the past, was very attentive and anticipated your needs. The server automatically replenished your drink and checked on you frequently, asking if you needed anything else. Because of his or her attentiveness, you left a big tip. Your tip "talked" to the server, saying "If you see this person again, do the same thing and you will be rewarded." You went back to the restaurant, the server did the same thing and you left a generous tip again. Money influenced you and the server.

You had the ability to leave a large tip and the server graciously received the blessing.

Each year, the American Psychological Association conducts a survey, polling Americans to see what people consider the major causes of stress. Not surprisingly, money was among the top stressors. The August 2017 survey revealed that sixty-two percent of respondents reported that money caused them stress and forty-five percent of them stated that they had lain awake at night due to stress.[ii]

While surveys conducted by others are informative indicators of the pulse of the nation, I wanted to see if this notion proved to be true in the church. A recent survey that I conducted among church-goers revealed that they, too, struggle with financial woes. Many of the those who took the survey were struggling to make ends meet, with forty-two percent of them living paycheck to paycheck. Like other survey takers, sixty-three percent of them responded that they had lost sleep because of finances. Forty percent of the respondents stated that they would not be able to make it if they did not receive their next paycheck on time. Clearly, the survey takers were not experiencing God's best.

Looking at these results, it is easy to understand why the Bible talks about money and material possessions. It has been stated that over 2000 verses in the Bible deal with money or material possessions and that one out of every ten verses in the New Testament deals with money.[iii] Jesus also talked about money and possessions in many of His parables because He knew that it was, is and will continue to be, a vital necessity that is sought after, misused and abused.

As mentioned in the opening paragraphs, God has a divine plan for us and our finances. If people are worrying, stressing, losing sleep and suffering from a lack of finances, then vital components of God's plan may be missing from their lives. They may not know God, they may not understand His plan, or they may refuse to follow His plan for finances. God's plan always works, but it is up to us to work His plan in order to find true success and peace. It's just like a recipe: you need to use the right ingredients, mix them according to the instructions and bake at the right temperature for the specified length of time. If you don't follow the recipe, you won't get the expected result.

When I was in college, I pledged a sorority. At the end of our pledge period, we had a block show, during which the pledges, sang songs about the sorority and danced (stepped) for the audience. For the block show, each of us had to wear a pants suit, which we were to make ourselves. I bought the material and pattern, cut the pieces according to the directions and began to sew. Wanting to finish the suit quickly, I failed to follow the directions fully. Consequently, the lapel on the jacket was not straight and the zipper in the pants was sewn in crooked. It was obvious that I had made a big mistake. I had to take the suit home to my mom, who took it apart, and properly reattached the pieces. While my ego was bruised when my mom looked at my mess and asked if I had read the directions, I was thankful that she took the time to dismantle my suit.

Because of my mom's intervention I was able to wear the suit and not look absolutely ridiculous. Sometimes, we mess up our lives the same way. But, our gracious, merciful God takes our lives, if we let Him, and remakes them so that we can become useful assets in His kingdom. God remakes our "suits," just like my mom remade the outfit for me. "And we know that all things work together for good to those who love God, to those who are the called according to His purpose" (Romans 8:28, NKJV).

God has given us His pattern and plan in the Bible, but many of us don't take the time to fully understand what His plan is, or follow it. There are some who have heard God's plan, but think that they only have to follow the part that best meets their fancy, sort of like my suit, only ending up back on the potter's wheel, having to be remade by God. To understand God's plan, you must spend time in the word of God – reading, meditating and listening to Him. Merely going to church on Sunday morning is not enough. You must purposefully seek Him, desiring the sincere milk of the Word to feed you and be the compass for your life.

Instead of drawing closer, it seems as though many are drifting from organized religion. It has been stated that church attendance is steadily declining and less than twenty percent of Americans regularly attend church on Sunday mornings, with many not belonging to a local congregation.[iv] Have we as a nation founded on the Christian faith lost our direction and strayed away from our roots? Could this be the reason why so many people are wandering around, facing trial after trial, trying to become prosperous without using the map that God has already prepared?

It is my intent for us to unveil God's plan and walk through it, applying God's principles in a way that is simple, practical and easy to apply in our lives. I invite you to come with me as we begin our journey to discover how God's plan works.

Chapter 1 — Things to Ponder

1. What does prosperity mean to you?

2. What is the abundant life that Jesus came to bring? Are you living the abundant life?

3. Money causes stress and loss of sleep for many people. Have you ever lost sleep because of money? Why?

4. What can you do to help you understand God's plan for you?

   _____
   _____
   _____
   _____
   _____

CHAPTER 2

God's Plan

> "Sometimes I haven't understood why he has done things and why things happened, but I know that God has a plan."
> — Jan Brewer

In the first chapter of Genesis, we read of how God created the heavens, the earth, and man. Genesis 1:26 states: "Then God said 'Let Us make man in Our image, according to Our likeness; let them have dominion over the fish of the sea, over the birds of the air, and over the cattle, over all the earth and over every creeping thing that creeps on the earth' " (NKJV). It further states in verse twenty-eight, "Then God blessed them, and God said to them, 'Be fruitful and multiply, fill the earth and subdue it; have dominion over the fish of the sea, over the birds of the air, and over every living thing that moves on the earth' " (NKJV).

Being made in the image of God, we have a body, a soul and a spirit. Jesus Christ is the bodily image of God, and we have the same physical form. Our soul, which consists of the mind, the will and emotions, makes us unlike any other creature on the earth. We have the ability to think, do and feel, just as God has those capabilities. Our spirit nature, the part of us that is renewed (born again) when we accept Christ as Lord and Savior, will live forever. We must be filled with, used by, and rely upon the Holy Spirit in order to truly live on this earth as God intended for us to live. The indwelling of the Holy Spirit occurs when we are born again, accepting Jesus Christ as our Lord and Savior. At that time, the Holy Spirit seals us for the day of redemption, making it impossible for anyone to snatch us out of God's hands.

Exactly what did God mean when He told Adam to "subdue" the earth? The Hebrew word for "subdue" is kabash, which means "to tread down, to conquer, to bring into subjection."[v] Dictionary.com defines subdue similarly, meaning "to conquer and bring into subjection, to overpower by superior force; overcome, to bring under mental or emotional control as by persuasion or intimidation; render submissive."

The Law of First Mention is a principle that many theologians use to determine the meaning of a word. Looking at other scriptures, they insert the meaning derived from the word as it was first used in the Bible to determine if their interpretation is truly accurate. Using the Law of First Mention, let's look at other scriptures in which the word subdue is used to determine if God really meant to say that man was to conquer and bring everything under subjection. In I Chronicles 17:8, God told David that He had been with him wherever he had gone, that He had made

David's name great and that God would subdue all of Israel's enemies. Surely enough, Israel conquered (subdued) their enemies with God's help. Psalm 47:3 says, "He will subdue the peoples under us, and nations under our feet." (NKJV). This, too, confirms that the definition of subdue means "to conquer, bring in subjection or control," as Israel conquered many nations and brought them under subjection.

2 Corinthians 13:1 says: "…By the mouth of two or more witnesses every word shall be established" (NKJV). Therefore, we can conclude from the Hebrew definition of subdue, the dictionary's definition and from applying the Law of First Mention, that God wants us to be in control of everything that is on the earth. Notice that I said that we are to have control over everything. This means that God relinquished the power to influence the affairs of the earth to man, giving man the ability to put all things under his feet. Therefore, God does not come down to earth, taking over everything. He works in and through man. That's why He sent Jesus in the form of a man to redeem us from the curse that resulted from Adam and Eve sinning in the garden.

Strong's Concordance gives the Hebrew word radah as the word for dominion. Radah means "to prevail against, reign, or rule." [vi] When I think of dominion, I think of a king and his kingdom. The king rules over the kingdom, the people are subjected to him, and they are under his control or authority. They must do as the king says. They must follow his rules, or face the consequences.

Revelation 1:4-6 says: "John, to the seven churches which are in Asia: Grace to you and peace from Him who is and who was and who is to come, and from the seven Spirits who are before His throne, And from Jesus Christ, the faithful witness, the firstborn from the dead, and the ruler over the kings of the earth. To Him who loved us and washed us from our sins in His own blood, and has made us kings and priests to His God and Father, to Him be glory and dominion forever and ever. Amen" (NKJV).

John noted that Jesus, our risen Savior, rules over the kings of the earth. The kings and priests referenced here are not those who hold such titles in designated countries or religious organizations. It refers to born again believers, those set apart by God to rule over earthly possessions. Believers have and should walk in dominion.

When God gave Adam dominion, He gave him and all believers in Christ three things:

1. Authority based upon the power of God
2. Access to the person of God
3. Anointing for the people of God

Satan knew the authority that God had given Adam and that is why he deceived Eve into eating the fruit. Because Eve had not been there when God commanded Adam not to eat the fruit from the tree of knowledge of good and evil, and she had received instructions second hand from

Adam, it was easier for Satan to make Eve doubt or question what God had said. As many know and have said, the mind is a battlefield in which Satan plants seeds of doubt and deception. If we concentrate on these thoughts they will grow into disbelief and rejection of the truth. After being deceived to eat of the fruit, Eve convinced Adam to eat as well. Then, Adam's and Eve's eyes were opened with knowledge of good and evil. Consequently, man and woman were cursed.

Because of Adam's sin, man has to toil to make a living. Eve caused a woman to be subject to her husband and bear pain in childbirth. Their fall caused us to suffer not only a physical death, but also a spiritual death, having a sin nature that separates us from God. To keep Adam and Eve from eating of the tree of life and living forever in a state of spiritual separation from God, God evicted them from the Garden of Eden.

By committing sin in the garden, Adam and Eve surrendered dominion, or control and authority, to Satan, making Satan the god of the world system. (See 2 Corinthians 4:3, 4; I John 5:19). But, God had a redemptive plan to save mankind through the precious blood of Jesus. Jesus recovered what had been lost in the Garden of Eden. Through Jesus' death and resurrection, man regained dominion. If we use the authority that is ours through Jesus, then we would truly live victorious lives.

As children of God, born again believers – those who have accepted Jesus as Lord and Savior – we have the authority to put anything and everything under our subjection, just as if God Himself had commanded it. Through God, we have the power to obtain and control our resources and be successful. Isaiah 48:17 says, "Thus says the Lord your Redeemer, the Holy One of Israel: 'I am the Lord your God Who teaches you to profit, Who leads you by the way you should go' "(NKJV). In Joshua 1:8, God told Joshua to not let the Book of the Law depart from his mouth, but to meditate upon it day and night; then Joshua would have good success. God was telling Joshua to keep thinking as the Word of God says to think and to keep saying what the Word of God says. By doing this, Joshua would have built his faith enough to do what the Word said he should do and he would be successful. Therefore, you and I must learn what God says about money and use money as God says we should use it. Only then will we find true financial success.

God also gave man access to Him. The devil wants us to believe that God is an angry, unforgiving God, who sits on His throne waiting for us to fail so that He can point His finger at us and say that He knew we were no good. This lie, from the pit of hell, is far from the truth. Through the blood of Jesus, we can walk into the Holy of Holies and talk to God personally. We are invited to come boldly to the throne of God to obtain mercy and find grace (Hebrews 4:16). We can call on God any time, and anywhere and He will hear us. Are you listening when He responds? Do you know His voice?

Several years ago, Creflo Dollar came to our church and preached about the anointing of God. He defined the anointing as "the burden removing, yoke destroying power of God." Yokes bind two things together. Yokes were used to connect two animals together so that they could walk in unison to plow or work. Yokes were a symbol of bondage. Jesus invites us to attach ourselves to Him and take His yoke upon us in exchange for the bondage that trials and tribulations place on us. In Matthew 11:28-30 He says: "Come to Me, all who labor and are heavy laden, and I will give you rest. Take My yoke upon you and learn from Me, for I am gentle and lowly in heart, and you will find rest for your souls. For My yoke is easy and My burden is light" (NKJV). When connected to Jesus, we will discover that God has given us the power to get and give wealth. Stressing over money, lying awake at night unable to sleep, is a yoke that no one wants as a harness. Jesus came to set the captives free. He came to give us rest, peace that surpasses understanding and a life free from worry. We need to let Him take care of us because He is more capable than any of us will ever be.

When God called Abraham, He told Abraham that He would make him a great nation and that He would bless Abraham to be a blessing (Genesis 12:2, 3). God wanted Abraham to be the conduit through whom others would be blessed. We find in Genesis 13:2, that Abraham was very rich, so God had indeed blessed him with material wealth as well as spiritual wealth. Because of Abraham's anointing and faith in God, we, his heirs by way of Jesus, are entitled to inherit the promises that God gave to him (Galatians 3:29). While everyone wants to stand in line to receive the good things that God has in store for us, not everyone wants to share or use those things as God desires. Unfortunately, many people erroneously think that what they purchased, have acquired or have possession of is theirs and is for their use only. That is far from the truth. God gives us dominion not only for ourselves but also for others. God gives us resources – gifts, talents, abilities, and yes, money – to benefit ourselves, help other people and build His kingdom. God gives us wealth so that we can have a part in establishing His covenant on the earth (Deuteronomy 8:18).

When the children of Israel were freed from bondage and left Egypt, they did not leave empty-handed. They asked the Egyptians for silver, gold, and clothes (Exodus 12:35, 36). The Egyptians gave them everything that they requested. In today's vernacular, the children of Israel wiped them out; they took it all. I know that many of you have seen the movie, *The Ten Commandments*. I remember the scene in the movie when the children of Israel left Egypt. They were weighed down with so much stuff that they could hardly carry it all. It is with that same depiction that

God wants us to look at ourselves in respect to His ability to bless and take care of us. If only we would let Him do it and not try to do it ourselves.

As the children of Israel traveled through the wilderness, God provided for them and met all their needs. He led them by a pillar of cloud during the day and a pillar of fire at night. He fed them manna, and their clothes and shoes did not wear out for the entire forty year period. In the sixteenth chapter of Exodus, Moses gave the people instructions on how they were to gather manna. Every morning the fine, round substance was on the ground and each household was to gather according to their need. There was to be nothing left over, whether they gathered a little or a lot. They were to gather one day's supply of manna each day for five days. On the sixth day, they were to gather a two-day supply, enough for days six and seven. They were to rest on the seventh day, just as God had rested when He created the earth, remembering the Sabbath.

Interestingly enough, there were some who did not listen. They failed to obey and follow the instructions Moses had given. There were some who gathered too much on days one through five, only to find the leftover manna stinking and full of worms the next day. There were some who did not gather enough on the sixth day, and went out on the seventh day to find nothing. Many Christians today are in the same predicament, finding themselves in a state of lack because they failed to follow God's directives and plans for their lives. They blame the devil and everyone else instead of looking at themselves. Job 36:11, 12 says "If they obey and serve Him, they shall spend their days in prosperity, and their years in pleasures. But if they do not obey, they shall perish by the sword, and they shall die without knowledge" (NKJV). God provided manna, but it was each person's responsibility to go out each day and gather the "bread" as instructed. It required work and obedience. God gives, but we must be diligent to seek, gather and use what He gives to us wisely. We cannot sit by idly and expect millions to fall from heaven into our laps. It won't happen. We must have a heart for God, desiring what He desires and doing as He commands.

God, our heavenly Father, has blessed us. We inherited His blessings through the shed blood of Jesus, but some people are running around, from church to church, trying to get "blessed." God is not our "Heavenly Lotto." You cannot run to church on Sunday, throw a couple of dollars in the offering bucket and expect to "hit" your blessing. It does not work like that. "If they obey and serve Him, they shall spend their days in prosperity, and their years in pleasures" (Job 36:11, KJV). Deuteronomy 5:33 says it even better, "Walk in obedience to all that the Lord your God has commanded you, so that you may live and prosper and prolong your days in the land you will possess" (NIV).

Chapter 2 — Things to Ponder

1. Define dominion.

2. What three things did God give us when he gave Adam dominion over the earth?

3. Define subdue.

4. How have you exercised dominion over your finances? Can you control the money that has been placed in your hands?

   _____
   _____
   _____
   _____
   _____

5. How does meditating on God's word help you?

   _____
   _____
   _____
   _____
   _____

6. Look at how Israel gathered manna. Do we have any responsibility in obtaining and walking in the prosperous life that God has for us?

   _____
   _____
   _____
   _____
   _____

CHAPTER 3

God is a God of Principles

> "Rules are not necessarily sacred, principles are."
> – Franklin D. Roosevelt

God is a God of principles. If we learn His principles—His ways of operation and methodologies, and diligently follow them—we will always prosper. Principles remain the same. They work the same way every time, for everybody. They do not change. They do not discriminate. God said that He does not change and the Bible teaches us that Jesus is the same yesterday, today and forever. If we follow Him and His ways, we will always find "good success." We must meditate on the Word of God, learn how to apply it to every aspect of our lives, using godly principles to find long-lasting success.

Just like all of you, I took math in school. I remember my Algebra II class in high school. We were taught certain algebraic equations and the teacher expected us to work through the correct formula step by step to reach the expected result. I didn't want to go through all the "unnecessary" steps that the teacher told us to follow because I could obtain the answers quicker by doing the calculations my way. Even though I had the right answer on one test, the teacher took points off because I did not follow the steps and directions that were given. I received ninety-eight percent, less than the best, because of my arrogance and disobedience. That's the way many of us are today. We fail to follow the steps and expect God's principles to work for us. We will never receive the full benefits of His promises if we push God aside and do it our way. We may reap a harvest, but it will be less than God's best.

I was upset about my score, so I asked to be taken out of the teacher's class. Because I didn't like him or the way he taught, I asked to be placed in an independent study class. I was given a book and I had to figure almost everything out by myself. My hard-headed nature caused me to take longer to solve problems that I did not understand initially. I had to sit in a class alone at times and wait for assistance when the overseeing instructor was not available to answer my questions. I completed the course and received an "A" as my final grade, but I did it the hard way.

Does this sound like your life? Have there been times when you could have had more or received a better result if you had just stopped to ask God for His instructions first, and followed them? Come on, you can confess, because I know I am not alone. Experience may be a great teacher, but it is easier and faster to follow the examples given by others. God has given us a road map – His Word. It is most expedient and profitable for us to follow it.

Many times, Christians don't know what rightfully belongs to them based upon promises God made to Abraham that were passed down to us, his heirs. Because of ignorance, which merely means lack of knowledge, they go through life barely making it, living without and in dire need. They did not know any better and had not been exposed to any other way of life except the one that they lived. We are not supposed to live below our privilege. Our heavenly Father owns everything, and He wants to share it with us.

You may have heard the story about a child who was watching her mother prepare a roast. When her mother chopped off the end of the roast prior to putting it in the pot, the child wanted to know why that was necessary. The woman informed the child that her grandmother had chopped off the end of her roasts the same way. Still curious, the child asked her grandmother why she chopped off the end of her roasts. The grandmother told her that a large roast would not fit in her pot, so she had to chop off the end. The woman had blindly followed a process that her mother used to cook a roast without understanding the reason why. The whole roasts would have fit her pot. Because of a lack of knowledge and understanding, she had thrown away perfectly good meat for years just because she failed to ask her mother for an explanation.

On Sunday, April 17, 2016, Lesley Stahl, correspondent for CBS News, aired a segment on 60 Minutes, entitled "Not Paid." In this segment, Ms. Stahl reported that many of the country's major insurance companies had failed to pay beneficiaries when the companies were aware that the insured person was deceased. [vii] Because beneficiaries were not aware of the policies or benefits that they were entitled to receive, the money was never claimed and remained with the companies. According to the news segment, most insurance companies were using the Social Security Death Master File to their advantage, to stop paying benefits on such things as annuities or retirement funds, but they did not use the information as notification to initiate a death claim. As a result of state investigations, many companies initiated processes to locate and pay policy proceeds to unsuspecting beneficiaries. If the beneficiaries cannot be located, the companies escheat the funds to the respective states.

Escheated funds can be held by the states for years before anyone comes forward to claim the benefits. Sometimes, beneficiaries never claim the money and the money still remains there, waiting for someone to come forward. Similarly, many Christians have benefits that have been "escheated," lying dormant and waiting to be claimed. These Christians are unaware of their inheritance. They live without the benefits that have been bought by the blood of Jesus and laid aside for them, just because they did not know what rightfully belongs to them. Just as one must follow the required steps to claim escheated funds and items from the states, Christians must follow God's processes and principles to claim what He has laid aside for us. It is well worth the effort to learn what God requires and obediently pursue His plan and purpose for our lives.

Several years ago, my husband received a phone call from his cousin who told him that he needed to call an attorney. This attorney had been looking for my husband for years, unable to find him. My husband grew up in one state, moved to another state after high school to go to college, then went on to another state before finally moving to Arkansas. To make things even more difficult, my husband had a common name which was not easily distinguished from others; there are hundreds of people in each of those states with the same name. After an exhaustive search, the attorney found my husband's cousin, who relayed the information to him.

My husband called the attorney and discovered that his great, great-grandfather had property from which my husband was entitled to receive mineral rights. The attorney sent a package that included his genealogy, a survey of the land, and the documents that needed to be completed in order to obtain what was his. My husband did not know about this land or his great, great-grandfather. Even though my husband was not aware of this part of his family, the land, or the mineral rights, he still was part "owner" because he was an heir. He never would have looked for this resource. After discovering what belonged to him, my husband still had to do his part. He had to follow through, complete the forms, get them notarized and then send them to the attorney. He could not receive any benefits until he had done what was required.

Some Christians don't know what God has set aside for them. The Bible provides our genealogy, going back to Abraham. Through the blood of Jesus, we are heirs to the promises that God gave to Abraham. We are blessed to be a blessing to others. We are to have all of our needs met and live in a wealthy place. Now, wealth does not mean that every Christian is going to be rich or a millionaire. However, it does mean that God intends for us to have more than enough and not live in poverty or from paycheck to paycheck as many people do. Like my husband or those who fail to claim escheated life insurance benefits, many are unaware of what belongs to them. As a result, they live below the privilege that God intended for them. We must trust God, and obediently follow HIs principles to "claim" what is ours as heirs according to the promises that were given to Abraham. People can't be like I was in my algebra class, expecting one hundred percent when we haven't followed the guidelines. If we are willing and obedient, we will eat the good of the land.

While there are some people who do not know what God has appropriated for them, there are still others who know what God has promised, but they want God to lay everything at their feet. Faith without works is dead, and we, as Christians, must be willing to do our part to inherit the promises of God. Reaping a harvest requires diligence and work.

God had led the children of Israel out of Egypt to the Promised Land, and He subdued their enemies making it possible for them to live freely in the place that they had been given. Yet, seven of the tribes of Israel failed to claim their inheritance. In the eighteenth chapter of Joshua, the people were scolded by Joshua because they had neglected to claim what was rightfully theirs and live freely in the Promised Land as God intended for them to live. Joshua sent three men from each tribe to survey the land and report their findings back to him. Then, he cast lots and allocated land to each of the seven tribes.

These seven tribes were negligent, too lazy to take the initiative to move further into the land and enjoy what belonged to them. Many Christians today are the same. They pray and ask God to bless them, then they refuse to go out and get what God has placed at their doorstep. Blessings can come in many forms, processes or phases. Financial prosperity may present itself through such things as your talent, opportunities, job, resources, vital connections to people or many other ways. God is not going to open heaven and drop one hundred dollar bills on us. We have to be ready and prepared to do the work to inherit the promise.

Galatians 4:1,2 states: "Now I say that the heir, as long as he is a child does not differ at all from a slave, though he is master of all, but is under guardians and stewards until the time appointed by the father" (NKJV). We may be required to mature in order to receive God's blessings. If we are not ready and prepared to handle the blessing, we may misuse, or lose what we have been given.

The world uses this same principle when it comes to minors receiving benefits that have been appropriated or set aside for them. Some people designate their minor children as beneficiaries of their life insurance policies. If the child is under the age of eighteen when the insured person dies, the benefits cannot be paid directly to him or her because the child lacks maturity and the ability to contract business. The money will remain with the insurance company until the minor turns eighteen, legal guardianship of the minor's estate is established by a person recognized by the courts, or until the company escheats the funds to the state. Even though the money belongs to the minor, it cannot be obtained without meeting the requirements.

God, likewise, holds or delays some of our blessings because He knows that we are not ready to receive them. The delays are not intended to penalize us, but to give us sufficient time to prepare to correctly use what God has in store. God wants us to mature and not remain as babes in Christ forever. If we do not grow up, demonstrating our ability to handle more, we can stifle God and limit our blessings.

In the book of Genesis we read about Joseph, Jacob's son, who was his father's favorite. Joseph was given a coat of many colors, and he was envied by his brothers. He and his brothers had such a strained relationship that they couldn't talk to each other peaceably. To make matters worse, Joseph flaunted his coat and wore it proudly around them. Though Joseph knew that his brothers envied him, he told them about a dream in which his brothers were bowing down to him. The dream caused his brothers to hate him even more. He had a second dream, more vivid than the first, in which he saw his parents and brothers bowing before him. The dreams enraged his brothers, and they sold Joseph into slavery.

While Joseph had been chosen by God to assist in the deliverance of Israel from famine, his character and maturity had to be developed to prepare him for his future. In the process of marching to his destiny, Joseph was enslaved, wrongly accused of a crime, and sent to prison before being placed in a position of authority in Egypt. Joseph needed to understand that some dreams must be kept in our hearts and not shared with everyone. There is a time and place for sharing them. Most times, the fulfillment of our dreams takes time and involves a process. Like Joseph, some of us need to grow up and mature so that we can walk in, live in and rest in the promises of God. The good thing about the process is that God never leaves or forsakes us.

Chapter 3 — Things to Ponder

1. What does it mean to you when we say that God is a God of principles?

   _____
   _____
   _____
   _____
   _____

2. Principles never change. Do you think that this is good or bad?

   _____
   _____
   _____
   _____
   _____

3. How are our blessings similar to unclaimed property?

   _____
   _____
   _____
   _____
   _____

4. Why are some of our blessings delayed or withheld?

   _____
   _____
   _____
   _____
   _____

5. What does living in a wealthy place mean to you?

   _____
   _____
   _____
   _____
   _____

6. List ways that financial blessings can be acquired?

   _____
   _____
   _____
   _____
   _____

CHAPTER 4

The Principles of Ownership and Stewardship

> "The earth is the Lord's and all its fullness, the world and those who dwell therein."
> – Psalm 24:1 (NKJV).

We have seen how money is on many people's minds, often affecting the quality of life that they live. The rich worry about keeping and growing their money, while the poor worry because they do not have enough. Neither of these groups has the right perspective. Both groups allow money to control their lives, when God should be the center. The Bible tells us not to worry about anything, but to go to God in prayer, letting Him know our need and thanking Him for His provision. Then, we will experience peace beyond understanding that cannot be explained (Phillipians.4:6, 7).

God owns everything and He has whatever we need. It does not matter what our need is, God has the answer and resources. Psalm 24:1 says "The earth is the Lord's and all its fullness, the world and those who dwell therein" (NKJV). God made us and we belong to Him (Psalm 100:3). He is the Creator and Owner of all that exists. As the Creator,

God made something out of nothing. Deuteronomy 10:14 further states: "Indeed heaven and the highest heavens belong to the Lord your God, also the earth and all that is in it" (NKJV). No one can possess anything that God did not own initially. We are stewards, or managers, of what He has allowed us to have in our possession.

A good steward oversees what has been placed in his possession as if it belongs to him. Because he values the possession, he takes care of it, makes improvements and watches over it to ensure that it is safe. God expects us to have this kind of mindset about every aspect of our lives.

When Adam and Eve sinned in the garden, they lost dominion and relinquished control of the earth to Satan, which resulted in mankind having a sin nature and becoming slaves to sin. Jesus came to redeem us from the bondage of sin and we became slaves of righteousness. Romans 6:21-23 states: "What consequences did you get from doing things that you are now ashamed of? The outcome of those things is death. But now that you have been set free from sin and become slaves to God, you have the consequence of a holy life and the outcome is eternal life. The wages that sin pays are death, but God's gift is eternal life in Christ Jesus our Lord" (CEB).

Because of Jesus, we have reestablished our relationship with God as our Father, and we are heirs of His kingdom. We have access to all that the Father owns and through faith and obedience, we can eat the good of the land. In and through Him, we have all that pertains to life and godliness. Every step we take, every breath we breathe and everything that we possess is a gift from God. He gives to us freely, and we are expected to freely give back to Him.

You may have heard the expression "possession is nine tenths of the law." This thought maintains that the person in possession of a thing is most likely the owner. However, possession and ownership are vastly different. Therefore, they should not be used interchangeably. Possession is temporary and the custody and control of the thing is subject to change. Ownership is permanent and provides a legal right to something. The owner maintains the rights to make changes to a deed, item or contract, even when the thing owned is not in his possession or custody.

Psalm 50:12 says, "If I were hungry, I would not tell you; For the world is Mine, and all its fullness" (NKJV). God owns everything and gives us all that is in our possession. As good stewards, we must use or sow the "seeds" – the resources, tools, skills and abilities that He has given to us – and commit to watch and wait in anticipation of the harvest. We must watch over the resources that God has given us, using faith to pull out the "weeds" or issues of life that may negatively impact us. We must ensure that the cares of this world do not strangle our good deeds and efforts, or cause us to ignore the Word and stray from God. In tough times, we should draw closer to God, not turn away. When the harvest is "reaped" and we receive money, assets, or resources, God expects us to give a portion to Him. Giving back to God should be done in faith, worship, and obedience to Him. It is not meant for us to hoard that which has been apportioned to us or use it all on ourselves. We need to look back, reach back and give back.

The Parable of the Minas, found in Luke 19:12-26, tells about a nobleman who traveled to a distant country. Prior to his departure, he called ten of his servants, distributed a total of ten minas, one mina to each servant, and instructed them to put the money to work until he returned. Upon his return, he called the servants to see if they had invested the money well. The first servant informed the nobleman that his mina had earned ten more. The second servant said that his mina had gained five more. The master commended both of these servants because they had been trustworthy and had increased what they had been given substantially. He placed the first servant in charge of ten cities and the second servant was given charge over five cities. Another servant came before the nobleman and returned the one mina that he had been given, saying that he had hidden it in a handkerchief because he was afraid of receiving negative repercussions from the master. In verse twenty-one, this servant told the master, "I was afraid of you, because you are a hard man. You take out what you did not put in and reap what you did not sow." (NIV). The master scolded the servant and asked him why he hadn't put the money in the bank, then it would have earned interest. He told the bystanders to take this servant's mina away and give it to the servant who had ten minas.

The Parable of the Minas differs from the Parable of the Talents. In this parable each servant was given the same amount of money. The master expected each servant to invest and increase what he had been given; and the servants expected the master to reap what he had not sown personally. Likewise, God gives to us and expects us to use our resources wisely, increasing them for the good of the Kingdom of God.

Just as the master gave each servant a mina, God gives each of us a measure of faith when we receive Christ as Savior (Romans 12:3). It is up to us to use our faith as we live and face the challenges of life. Using faith increases our confidence in God and willingness to stand on His promise to move mountains that we face in our lives. If we fail to use faith, the enemy comes in, steals what we have and subjects us to fear. The servant who hid his mina did not use his faith; instead, he allowed fear of failure to jeopardize his future. God requires us to use our faith to live and to go forward, giving God the glory for all that He has done. Without faith, it is impossible to please God.

Having the kind of faith that moves mountains is not easy. It takes determination and perseverance. When we start believing God for anything, we are full of faith in the initial stages. As time goes by and the thing that we requested does not materialize, our faith tends to wane. The enemy waits for this moment so that he can come in and wreak havoc in our lives. The devil will destroy our lives and our hopes, if we give up and give in. Our faith must be focused on the finish line and what God has promised in His word. We must see ourselves as victorious. Myles Monroe once said "If what you see is not what you saw, then what you see is temporary." In other words, "Faith is the reality of what we hope for, the proof of what we don't see" (Hebrews 11:1, CEB). Know that detours, disappointments and delays don't change our destiny. They only alter how we get there. We must press in and press on, in Jesus' name.

All of us have used toothpaste and are familiar with the way the paste is packaged. When we first get the tube of toothpaste, we can squeeze any place on the tube and the toothpaste will come out. As the amount of toothpaste in the tube decreases, we must become more deliberate about where and how we press the tube. It takes more force to squeeze the tube when it is getting empty, and the pressure must be steady and consistent. Most of us have a technique for getting the last of the toothpaste from the tube. We start from the bottom and sometimes we may even roll the tube up so that it forces the remaining toothpaste to the top. I have even had times when I pressed the tube so hard that a small hole opened on the side of the tube. This unexpected opening provided enough toothpaste to meet my immediate need until I could get to the store to buy more.

In time of need, we must apply faith for the requested thing in the same manner as we do when getting that last bit of toothpaste. Press in. Use the unchanging Word and principles of God, knowing that the answer is there. When we have unwavering faith, God will not only meet the need. Many times He will open doors that we did not expect to open. Just as pressure forces toothpaste out of a tube when we least expect it, God moves suddenly and in ways that we do not anticipate. We must trust and keep on pressing in. The next time your faith is tested and you are tempted to give up, "brush your teeth!" The Holy Spirit will let you know that God has not forgotten you.

Chapter 4 — Things to Ponder

1. What is the difference between ownership and possession?

2. In the Parable of the Minas, why was the mina taken from the servant who had one?

3. Are you accountable for the gifts, talents, resources and abilities that God has given you? What are you expected to do with them?

4. How does the Parable of the Minas differ from the Parable of the Talents?

5. What must you do when the thing for which you have prayed has not materialized?

God's Mighty Dollar

CHAPTER 5

The Principle of the Tithe

> "I never would have been able to tithe the first million dollars I ever made if I had not tithed my first salary, which was $1.50 per week."
> – John D. Rockefeller

Making the decision to tithe is difficult for many Christians. This challenge stems from people's hearts. They must truly trust God as the owner of everything and fully believe that He will take care of them better than they can take care of themselves. Statistics show that only three to five percent of Americans tithe to their local church. Of those who tithe, only seventeen percent of them do so regularly.[ix] It is easier to tithe when we are taught and begin this practice of honoring God at an early age. Because the income is smaller when we are young, giving does not seem to be as much of a challenge. As people make more money, they tend to look at the overall dollar amount and think that it is too much to give to the church, or as some say, "that pastor." The dollar amount is not the issue, as the impact should be the same no matter how much you make.

There are several things that affect the hesitancy to tithe. They include a lack of understanding of the principle of tithing, fear, and arrogance. Many churches do not teach or stress tithing today. Consequently, the members are unaware of the significance of tithing or the benefits of honoring God first with their finances. In these times when it is difficult to get people to go to church, some pastors shy away from anything that would offend those who do come. Also, because many in church leadership believe that tithing was only practiced under the law and we are now under grace, they erroneously conclude that tithing is not for today. Therefore, their congregants are misinformed and are not given the opportunity to see God's plan for their finances work. Still other churches merely invite tithers to come to the front to place their tithes in a special box and receive a prayer. These people then parade in front of others to proudly display the fact that they are different from everyone else.

Fear of losing what you have, fear of not having enough, and fear of relinquishing control to someone else are reasons why some people may not tithe. Fear is the opposite of faith, and it causes people to look at the situation rather than looking at God and what His Word says. The Bible teaches us to walk by faith and not by sight (2 Corinthians 5:7). The attitude of faith is that no matter what it looks like, if we trust God and give as He commands, He will supply our needs.

People are arrogant when they think they know how to handle the money that is in their possession better than anyone else, including God. This attitude of self-sufficiency and importance causes them to think that they worked for their money and it belongs to them, so they believe they can do whatever they want or need to do with it.

There are arguments galore about the tithe and whether or not it is applicable today. In recent months, I have even heard pastors of large churches dispute the significance of tithing. They contend that we are under grace, and God does not require us to tithe as He did under the law. People who question the relevance of the tithe really don't want to do it. They don't have the heart to fully serve and commit all that they have to God because they do not see God as the owner of everything they have. Listed below are some of the reasons I have heard people use as justification for not tithing as God prescribes.

- Tithing was a part of the law and we are under grace.
- I can't afford to tithe.
- Tithing is not in the New Testament.
- The New Testament tells us to give according to our heart.
- The Bible does not tell us to tithe a specific amount.
- Tithing should be based on what I have left over, the net income and not the gross income.
- God doesn't expect me to give what I don't have.

- I worked hard for this money and I should determine how to spend it. It's my money.
- The tithe does not have to go to the church. As long as I give it to meet a need, I am giving to God's cause.

The principle of tithing was first introduced in the book of Genesis, before the Law. Lot, Abram's nephew, had been captured following a battle between kings of multiple cities. They had taken Lot, his family and all of his possessions. When Abram heard about this, he took his servants with him and they attacked the kings who had captured Lot. After Abram defeated the kings, he returned home and Melchizedek, the king of Salem, brought him bread and wine. Melchizedek also was a priest and is symbolic of Christ. In essence, the pre-incarnate Christ came to have communion with Abram when Melchizedek came with bread and wine. Abram gave Melchizedek a tithe of all that he had (Genesis 14:20). Grateful that he had retrieved his family, Abram wanted to honor Melchizedek, the high priest, with the tithe. He was not commanded to do this.

The word tithe means "tenth" and is symbolic of being whole and complete. There are multiple instances throughout the scriptures that indicate the number ten as a reflection of completeness. In the first book of Genesis, we see the words "God said" ten times. God sent ten plagues on Egypt. There were ten bridesmaids and ten lepers. In fact the numeric system is based upon sets of ten.

In the twenty-eighth chapter of Genesis, Jacob had a dream of a ladder reaching heaven and angels were ascending and descending it. God spoke to Jacob and revealed how He was going to bless Jacob and his descendants. Realizing the magnitude of the dream, Jacob made a vow to give a tenth (tithe) of what he had to God. Throughout the books of Leviticus, Numbers, Deuteronomy, 2 Chronicles, Nehemiah, and Amos, God gave more instructions regarding the tithe. Though the tithe was introduced prior to the law, I believe that God included the tithe as part of the law to stress the value and significance that it can and should have in our lives. The relevance and impact of tithing was not abolished with the commencement of the New Covenant and implementation of grace.

In Matthew 23:23, Jesus admonished the scribes and Pharisees about their actions. He told them that they needed to practice justice, mercy and faithfulness in addition to giving their tithes. Therefore, arguments that tithing was a part of the law and is not in the New Testament are incorrect. The Pharisees were tithing in the New Testament, but their hearts were not filled with the love of God. Jesus was telling them that giving out of habit and not from the heart means little. We should love, honor, and trust God so much that we willingly give back to Him joyously.

2 Corinthians 9:6, 7 reads as follows, "But this I say: He who sows sparingly will also reap sparingly, and he who sows bountifully will also reap bountifully. So let

each one give as he purposes in his heart, not grudgingly or of necessity; for God loves a cheerful giver" (NKJV). These verses have been misused and abused by proponents against tithing. They argue that God merely wants us to give from our hearts freely and joyfully and that the tithe is not necessary or required. While the principle of sowing and reaping applies to every aspect of life, in this scripture Paul was not talking about the tithe. Paul was writing to the Corinthians concerning gifts that they had promised to give to others who were in need. Paul was asking the Corinthians to give whatever was in their hearts and to do it freely. If we think about the fact that God owns everything, giving Him ten percent and keeping the other ninety percent for our personal use should be a no brainer.

Though it is not stated in the Bible, some people believe that the principle of the tithe began in the Garden of Eden and that the tree of the knowledge of good and evil represented the tithe. God told Adam that he could eat freely from every tree in the garden except the tree of the knowledge of good and evil. God said that Adam would die the day that he ate of that tree. After Eve was ensnared by Satan, she and Adam ate from the tree. Immediately, they were cast from the garden to keep them from eating of the tree of life and living eternally separated from God.

Mankind has suffered many consequences resulting from Adam's and Eve's sin. Satan planted doubt and disbelief in Eve's mind, which caused her to question whether God really meant what He said. Her willingness to sin affected Adam and they plunged into sin together. Today, many people "eat" their tithe. They use the resources that should have been allocated to God as their own. Because they fail to acknowledge God, they do not walk in the abundant life that God intended for them to receive.

In Malachi 3:10, God challenges us by saying, "Bring all the tithes into the storehouse, that there may be food in My house. And try Me now in this, says the Lord of hosts, if I will not open for you the windows of heaven and pour out for you such blessing that there will not be room enough to receive it" (NKJV). This is the only place in the Bible where God tells us to test Him to prove that He is a God of His Word. God wants us to bring the tithe to the church, His house, not give it to someone else or support some other outside cause. No matter how worthy or deserving a person or cause may be, the tithe should not be given to them. While it is good to support and assist others, the tithe should never be used for those purposes. Offerings and alms are given to the poor and others.

Because we know that God owns everything and that all of our possessions come from Him, we should be able to easily give back. Notice that God instructs us to bring the tithes to the storehouse. We do not pay tithes. We give back what belongs to God. You may have worked hard, moved up the ladder and received a big corporate paycheck, but you wouldn't have been able to do it without God. Everyone has been given something, some greater amounts, others lesser amounts. Regardless of the amount, we should give back proportionately. Remember the parable of the talents, the five, two and one talent. While the servants were given differing amounts, each was expected to have something to give back. The same goes for you and me. The question is, what have you done with what you have been given?

Those who say that they don't have anything to give have chosen to walk by sight and not by faith. Though a person may have limited resources, God still asks us to trust Him and give Him the opportunity to supply our needs. I have seen God open windows for us. One company for which I worked lost a major government contract and consequently I was one of over 500 people who were laid off. I received a small severance and I was eligible for unemployment benefits, but the amounts were a far cry from my salary. We had two small children, a mortgage, car payments and other bills to pay. It was a challenging time financially, and we were tempted not to give to the church just as many other people are tempted. However, God showed us something during those times that I will never forget.

My husband had a small company that he ran on the side, outside of his regular job. He had received a few jobs from a county agency that brought in a small amount of money, but nothing in comparison to the income that we had lost from my job. One day, Don received a call from a county manager who asked if he was able to do a job for him. The job required someone to work full time as an independent contractor for the County of Milwaukee updating end user procedures. Since Don could not leave his fulltime job for a temporary position and I did not have a job, he told me that I had to do it. The problem was, I had no idea what an end user was.

I dressed up in a suit, carried my briefcase and notebook; and did not say a word when we met with the county manager. I just smiled and looked like I knew what he and Don were discussing. The manager gave us the contract, making $60.00 an hour. (You know that had to be God's intervention.) I worked with another contractor from California, and we updated volumes and volumes of procedures. When I did not know or understand the technical language I asked the other contractor or called Don and he answered my questions. God opened the windows of heaven and poured out a blessing that was unimaginable. I worked three months and made more money than I would have made in one year on my job.

This happened in 1986. Sixty dollars an hour would have been $124,800 a year in 1986 if it had been equated to working on a full time job. Factoring for inflation, I would have made $281,483.95 a year if this happened in 2018. I did not make $281,483.95 on my job. In fact, my salary was nowhere near that much. God provided exceedingly, abundantly above all that we could ask or think.

The tithe should be set aside before anything else is done with your money. If this is done, God has promised to demonstrate and prove His trustworthiness by blessing you. Recently, I challenged a relative to tithe. He decided to give it a try and right after he gave his tithe, someone followed him as he left the church and gave him some money, just to bless him. He was excited to see God move. The person who gave him the money did not know that my relative had just given a tithe. Of course, this is not to say that every time you give, someone will give you some money right away. But when we are obedient, God does reciprocate. God's plan always works. We just have to work His plan.

If you say that you can barely make it and your bills are overdue, God has an answer for that, too. We are to trust Him, prove Him and see what He will do for us. When my husband and I first came into the knowledge of tithing we, like many others, were deeply in debt. We "couldn't afford to tithe" but we knew it was right according to the Word of God. Our hearts were right, but our faith was small, so we set out to "prove" God by building our faith to trust Him and tithe as He instructed. When we first decided to tithe during the early years of our marriage, we should have been giving $50 per week. We were only giving $25 at that time and even that was a stretch. We decided to build our faith by increasing our giving in $5 increments. We increased our weekly offering to $30 and found that we were able to do it. Then we increased to $35, then $40, then $45, until we reached $50 per week. This process took us a couple of months, but as we were building our faith we learned to trust God at each level. After reaching the $50 weekly tithe, we had grown to know and understand that God's principle worked. We tested God, and He proved how He works. We lacked nothing. As our salaries increased, so did our tithe, always based on giving ten percent of gross income. When we sat down to list our bills, we always listed the tithe first.

In order for tithing to work as God prescribes, it must be done consistently. Statistics have shown that only seventeen percent of Americans state that they regularly tithe.[x] We cannot hit-and-miss, giving as we feel like it or giving as it is convenient for us. To receive the blessings, tithing must be a way of life. If you miss a Sunday, you are supposed to send your tithe or give the missed tithe in addition to your current tithe when you return. Actually, the Bible says that you should add twenty percent for the missed tithe (Leviticus 27:31). If you only give as it is convenient to you, then you aren't putting God first. When you don't tithe consistently, you are not really a tither and you are deceiving yourself. You will not receive the promised blessing if you do not tithe consistently by bringing it first before paying any other bills. Because people fail to tithe or even give at all, many churches are suffering. People say that they get tired of the preachers begging for money.

If every church member honors God and gives consistently, then pastors would not have to ask for any additional offerings. This leads me to another thing—those who say that they are not going to give their money to "that preacher," making him rich. When the tithe is released and given to the church, in obedience to God, you are not responsible for it. There is no need to worry about how it is allocated or used. Hebrews 7:4-8 tells us that Abraham gave a tenth. The law required his descendants to give the tenth to the Levites and that we give our tithe to One Who is greater—Jesus. The important fact is that you will be blessed because you honored God. If the pastor misappropriates what has been given to the church, then he will have to answer for it, not you. Let God handle the pastor and anyone else who misappropriates church funds. It's not your responsibility, nor is it a legitimate reason not to tithe.

We see new Christians who learn about the tithe, believe that it is right and decide to start tithing immediately. Because their debt is high and bills are due, they discontinue tithing when challenges come their way. Their faith is not strong enough to resist the devil. James 4:7 gives advice for these types of situations. It says: "Therefore, submit to God. Resist the devil and he will flee from you" (NKJV). Submitting to God is the vital key that provides the strength needed to fight the enemy. It will take determination and commitment, but if you hang in there, you will receive the promise. If your faith is not strong enough to fully commit, then progressively increase the amount of your giving as my husband and I did. Building faith is a process in which we must learn how to trust God. God always does His part; hang in there and do your part.

We have talked about people who think they can't afford to tithe because they have insufficient money to pay all of their bills. Sometimes the inability to pay bills occurs because people misappropriate the resources they have been given. The availability of credit is quick and easy. We receive offers in the mail, via email, and even at the cashier's desk in the department stores. All it takes is the quick completion of an application to receive almost instant access to money. This new money makes it easy to have everything our hearts desire, without ever needing to wait.

We often think that if the Joneses next door can have it, so can we. We buy things as status symbols, whether we can afford them or not, trying to get someone else to think that we are "blessed." Look at how many families are buying their sons the latest brand-name tennis shoes, even though they had to buy the shoes on credit. They pay twenty-five percent interest or more, so that their sons can be accepted by peers. Don't forget the parents who buy expensive cars to impress others.

In Arkansas, the sales tax on new cars is paid when the license plate is issued. Many people drive around with expired temporary tags because they cannot afford to pay the sales tax and get their license plates. If you cannot afford to pay the tax, then you cannot afford the car. Stop trying to impress others. Do what you can do where you are. With time, you can get to where you want to be. People need to think about their priorities and put them in the proper perspective. I am not saying that it is wrong to buy shoes or an expensive car, because God gives us all things richly to enjoy. I am saying that you cannot trust in those things or depend upon them for happiness or to determine your worth. True happiness comes from God.

You may have to wait to get some of the things you want because you are not mature enough to appreciate what God does for you. It also may be that you need discipline to control spending excessively on things that have no real value. I started to receive credit card applications in the mail when I was in my fourth year of college. I was excited because I was ready to be grown up, with my own credit. I applied for credit cards, with no job and only hopes of a future. I was issued several cards and I thought that I was on my way. I remember buying a leather coat and charging it on my Master Card. The bill came and I only paid the minimum. There were some months when I didn't have the money to pay the minimum and I called my brothers and sisters to obtain the money. I didn't want to tell my parents because they gave me a monthly "allowance" which I had already wasted. I should not have had that credit card and I most definitely should not have used it to purchase something that was not necessary.

Though I could walk around the grounds of the university and look stylish, I was financially broke and unable to pay my bill. My focus was on the wrong things. "Do not store up for yourselves treasures on earth, where moths and vermin destroy, and where thieves break in and steal. But store up for yourselves treasure in heaven, where moths and vermin do not destroy, and where thieves do not break in and steal. For where your treasure is, there your heart will be also" (Matthew 6:19-21, NIV). Put God first and He will give you everything you need, without the stress that credit cards give. Just a note—that leather coat has been gone for years. I went through months of stressing over making payments for something that did not last.

There is much dispute over whether the tithe should be based upon the gross income or the net income. The terms "gross" and "net" income are not used in the Bible. Your gross income is the amount that you make before anything is deducted. The money that you bring home from your job after deductions is your net income. Net income is the portion that remains after you have paid taxes, insurance, and any other deductions. If Jesus said we should seek the kingdom first, then the government and its taxes, your insurance, 401K, the Christmas club or anything else should not take precedence over the tithe. Matthew 6:33 tells us to seek first the kingdom of God and His righteousness and all other things will be given to us. I don't think that God wants us to be so legalistic when it comes to showing reverence and honor to him. If we truly love Him, then it should not be a question of tithing off the gross or net. Tithing off the gross would be done without hesitation. So, if you want more, why don't you give more? He has promised to open the windows of heaven and pour out a blessing, so we always win.

It has been found that people who tithe are better stewards of their money, with many having little or no credit card debt. They are doing just as much or more with ninety percent of their income as compared to those who are using one hundred percent of their income. This is evidence that people who tithe are receiving the blessings that God promised.

Chapter 5 — Things to Ponder

1. How much is the tithe?

2. Can the tithe be given to anyone or to any organization?

3. List five reasons why people refuse to tithe.

4. What did God promise to do when we choose to tithe?

5. Was tithing implemented before or after the Law?

6. Why do you think that God included tithing as part of the Law?

7. When you tithe, what do you demonstrate to God?

8. Do you think that you should tithe on gross or net income? Why?

_____
_____
_____
_____
_____

CHAPTER 6

The Principles of Saving and Investing
Responsible Choices

> "The philosophy of the rich and the poor is this:
> the rich invest their money and spend what is left.
> The poor spend their money and invest what is left."
> – Robert Kiyosaki

Earlier, I quoted Psalm 24:1, which states that the earth and everything in it belong to God. Consequently, we are to be good stewards of the things God has entrusted to us. As good stewards of the resources God has given us, we are expected to use these resources properly, give, save, and invest.

"The wise have wealth and luxury, but fools spend whatever they get" (Proverbs 21:20, NLT). More often than not, people fail to save and put aside for the future. There are some who say they can't afford to save because they barely have enough to meet their needs. Others think that saving is a signal that you are not depending upon God. Still others purposely choose to live their best life now, and not prepare for tomorrow. The Bible tells us that we should save and also demonstrates how this should be done in preparation for future needs.

In the forty-first chapter of Genesis, Pharaoh had a dream, which was interpreted by Joseph. In the dream, Pharaoh saw seven healthy cows, and then saw seven lean, ugly cows, which ultimately ate the seven fat, healthy cows. He had another dream and saw seven heads on a full stalk followed by the sight of seven blighted stalks. Joseph informed Pharaoh his dreams indicated that Egypt was going to experience seven years of plenty, followed by seven years of very severe famine. Joseph advised Pharaoh to appoint a wise man over Egypt to store grain in preparation for the years of famine. Pharaoh chose Joseph for this task.

We, like Egypt, will face ups and downs in life. There will be times when everything we touch will appear to turn into gold, as the saying goes, and then at other times the bottom may seem to fall out, leaving us in need. To prepare, we are advised to save, just as God alerted Pharaoh in his dream. We cannot wait until there is a problem and expect resources to be available if we have not prepared in advance.

Last year, right before Christmas, I had to buy new tires. I had purchased a new car several years ago and the original tires had worn down and needed to be replaced. Now, I could have blamed the devil as many Christians do, saying that the enemy caused this to happen. This response would indicate that I did not take responsibility and did not adequately prepare for what should have been expected. When I bought the car, I should have known that the car would depreciate and that the parts would wear out eventually. Nothing on this earth will last forever. It was my responsibility to either set aside the funds or have money already available to meet the expected need. I was able to purchase four new tires with no strain or struggle.

To understand the investment principle, let's look at the Parable of the Talents found in the twenty-fifth chapter of Matthew. In this parable, the traveler, or lord, called his servants together and informed them that he was going away. He gave to each person, according to his ability. To the first servant he gave five talents. Two talents were given to the second servant and the third servant received one talent.

A talent could be made of gold or silver and had the potential of being worth a lot of money. I have seen various estimates of the value of a talent ranging from several hundred dollars to over one million, depending upon the weight of the talent. Regardless of which figure you choose to believe, it is safe to say that each servant was given a significant amount of money. The servants were not told what to do with the money, but there must have been an expectation for each servant to handle the talent(s) responsibly because the servants had to settle accounts with the traveler when he returned. The servants were to take what they had been given and make it increase by investing it wisely, thus adding value to the traveler's resources as well as theirs.

When the traveler returned, he found that the servant who had been given five talents gained five more talents, the servant with two talents increased his by two, and the servant with one talent hid his talent, fearing that he would lose it. Consequently, that servant gained nothing. The servants who had invested their talents were given accolades and the lord (traveler) gave them even more, allowing them to oversee or rule many things. The servant who had hidden his talent was scolded and that which he had was taken away and given to the servant who had increased his talents to ten. Through this parable, we are taught several things:

1. God distributes to each of us according to our ability to handle the resources.
2. God holds us accountable and responsible for everything that He gives us.
3. God expects us to use our faith, step out and invest what He has given us.
4. God rewards and penalizes us for the decisions that we make with the finances that have been given to us.

God knows us better than we know ourselves. He knows our strengths, weaknesses, gifts and abilities. He gives us what we can handle and according to our faithfulness. God knew that the person to whom He had given five talents was capable of doing the greatest things and the person with one talent did not have the same skill set, but that servant was still expected to utilize what he had. Many times people want to make excuses and blame others for their non-performance. The servant with one talent in essence blamed the lord for the lack of increase, saying that he hid the talent because he did not want to be held responsible for losing it.

All of us will have to give an account of our actions and will receive rewards accordingly. I Corinthians 3:9-15 tells us that each man's work will be tested, tried by fire, and that if the person's work endures, he will receive a reward. If the work is burned, he will suffer loss. Though we are saved by grace through faith in Jesus and not by our works, we are still expected to be obedient and do good work (Ephesians 2:8-10).

The principle of saving is also demonstrated through the activities of the ant. Proverbs 6:6-8 tells us: "Go to the ant, you sluggard! Consider her ways and be wise, which, having no captain, overseer or ruler, provides her supplies in the summer, and gathers her food in the harvest" (NKJV). The ant, though small and seemingly insignificant, is wise enough to set aside food and resources for the difficult times. It does not have to be told what to do. The ant does not get excited when it sees abundance. Instead, it prepares for the lean season that is destined to come and sets aside a little at a time.

Have you ever looked at ants? I have seen ants that have lifted pieces of food that were very large, compared to their size. The ants struggled along, slowly moving toward their place of storage. Knowing that summer will not last forever and the scarcity of winter will make it hard for them to find food, they set aside food when they have an abundance. When winter comes, and food is scarce, ants go to their storage and find what is sufficient to meet their needs. We should be like-minded. Begin saving a little at a time, setting aside change or a couple of dollars if that is all you have. Consistently taking small steps gradually builds a reserve. While you may not have a million dollars overnight, with diligence, the money will grow.

There are major areas that we need to consider when saving and investing. The first is an emergency fund. Life will always bring unexpected things—the emergency car repairs, sickness, breakdown of appliances, and the list goes on. If you don't have one, you need to establish an account that you can tap into whenever these types of things occur. One thousand dollars seems to be the golden amount that most people strive to attain first. That may seem like a million dollars if you do not have anything now. Again, the object is to start somewhere.

The best way to save is to have it deducted from your check automatically and deposited into a savings account. I started by setting aside a small amount from my weekly $20 allowance that I gave myself many years ago. I would stuff $5 or $10 in an envelope each week, and I was amazed when I looked in there and found that I had accumulated several hundred dollars. Then, I proudly opened a savings account that was used for emergencies and the little extravagances that every girl enjoys.

Long term savings for retirement are also important. When you are young, you may think that you have all the time in the world to do this and decide to wait until later to start. The time to start saving for retirement should begin when you get your first "real" job after graduating from high school or college. Each year the government determines the maximum amount that you can invest into retirement accounts prior to taxes. Investing in 401K, 403B or other pre-tax retirement plans offered by employers is a great option. If your job offers a retirement plan, you should invest at least the amount that the company matches. So, if the company offers one hundred percent match up to six percent of your salary, you should invest at least six percent of your salary to obtain the double return. If you can invest more than the amount that the company matches, then that is advisable. Those who waited a little late to start saving for their retirement may be eligible to "catch-up" and invest more than the annual limit, if they are age fifty or over.

Don't make the mistake and think that you can't afford to invest into pretax retirement plans. It really doesn't have as much of an impact on your take home pay as you may imagine. Because the remaining income is lower, the tax incurred is less, thereby reducing the overall impact on take home pay.

The government allows you to invest up to a specific amount into retirement plans each year. For example, in 2019, the maximum contribution is $19,000. The catch up contribution is $6,000. Therefore, a person of fifty years or older could save up to $25,000 in pretax dollars. If you are under fifty, and you invest less than $19,000, increase your contributions as much as you can. When you receive your annual increase on your job, increase your contribution by at least one percent each year until you reach the maximum allowable contribution. You won't miss the money, because you never had it. You will be surprised at how well this works and you will reap the returns when you retire.

Retirement savings can be accumulated through Individual Retirement Accounts (IRAs). You can have a traditional or Roth IRA. A tax advisor will be able to tell you the advantages of both and which would benefit you most.

Investments such as stocks and mutual funds aren't as unattainable as you may think. There are multiple ways to purchase stocks through many internet sites. Some companies will deduct money from your checking account each month to purchase their stock. The point is to start somewhere and build. My husband and I purchased our first stock years ago, at $3 per share when we didn't have a lot of money. We eventually sold that and purchased other stock and took the dividends to purchase more stock. In that way, we kept growing the investments.

I have seen so many people, both young and old, who did not have life insurance or who only had life insurance through their jobs. If they lose their jobs, the term life insurance that the employer offers ends immediately. If they don't have a separate policy that they purchased directly from an insurance company, they would have nothing. When young, people make the mistake of thinking they are invincible and will live forever. They fail to effectively prepare for tomorrow. The best time to purchase insurance is when you are healthy and young. Then you can buy more insurance for a lower premium.

Term life insurance is the simplest and cheapest type of life insurance policy. These policies have periods of coverage (the term period) for designated lengths of time, such as five, ten, and fifteen years or more. Term policies are very cheap, if purchased when you are young, and you can get tens of thousands of dollars in coverage for a nominal amount. The drawback for term policies is that the premiums increase after each term period ends, making them very expensive when you reach retirement age. It is wise to purchase a term policy when you are young and have a family to support, getting maximum coverage for a small amount. You then have the opportunity to invest additional money somewhere else so that it will grow and be available for you later when the premium on the term policy rises and becomes unaffordable. By that time, children are usually grown and out of the house, so the need to provide for a growing family is not as great.

Permanent life insurance policies, many of which mature at age ninety-five, consist of policies such as universal life, whole life, variable life and others that build cash value. These policies have higher premiums, and they allow you to get loans from the cash value which you do not have to pay back. However, the loans do accrue interest that must be paid every year. If you choose not to repay the loans, they are deducted from the face amount of the policy when you die and the beneficiary receives the remaining amount. The premiums on these policies usually remain the same. Some of these policies also allow you to use accumulated value to pay premiums. Be sure to discuss these policies fully with an agent and read your policy carefully upon receipt.

There is one more thing. Parents should not forget to purchase life insurance for their children. Many companies offer child term riders (CTRs) that can be attached to the parent's policy. The CTRs are very cheap, and most allow you to purchase coverage on dependent children until they are at least eighteen. Once insured, some cover dependent children until they are twenty-five. When the child is no longer a dependent, he or she can convert to an individual policy. Talk to an agent today if you do not have coverage.

While we hate to think about our children dying prior to us, unfortunately it can and does happen, as I know very well.

Buying a home is the center of the American dream and most people consider it as an investment. While you may build equity in your home over time, it is still a liability or financial obligation until you pay for it in full. Of course, the annual taxes on your home will always have to be paid. Owning a home also comes with the need for upkeep and repairs. It can be a great expense. Additionally, equity that is in the house is not readily accessible in time of need. The positive thing about owning a home is that the mortgage interest and real estate taxes are deductible from income taxes. But even so, you could save more if there were no mortgage at all. That is when we really feel free to live, save and give to the utmost.

Chapter 6 – Things to Ponder

1. Why should we save and invest?

2. What can we learn from the ant?

3. What does the Parable of the Talents teach you?

4. List some ways that you can set aside savings.

5. What is the advantage of purchasing term life insurance?

6. What is a cheap way to purchase term life insurance on your children?

God's Mighty Dollar

CHAPTER 7

The Principles of Sowing and Reaping
The Law of Divine Reciprocity

> "Someone is sitting in the shade today because someone planted a tree a long time ago."
> – Warren Buffett

The principle of sowing and reaping, also referred to as seedtime and harvest, was instituted when God created the earth. God placed seeds in herbs, trees, animals, man and other creations, giving them the ability to reproduce. The word "seed" is also used generally in reference to anything that is sown. We give or sow seeds with every thought, action, word, thing or deed. We sow good, bad, love, hate, kindness, joy, forgiveness, time, money and so much more. Sowing and reaping is understood universally and will exist forever. "While the earth remains, seedtime and harvest, cold and heat, winter and summer, and day and night shall not cease" (Genesis 8:22, NKJV).

The Law of Divine Reciprocity includes a supernatural aspect that magnifies and multiplies the return that is received when we give anything according to the Word of God. Reciprocity involves an exchange between two people or entities for mutual benefit. When we sow as God mandates, we receive much more than we could gain had He not been involved. We must make decisions about how to sow, where to sow, what to sow and when to sow. With God, the principle of sowing and reaping has many attributes that the world does not and cannot replicate.

The primary financial principle of sowing is found in the tithe, which we discussed earlier. God demonstrates the Law of Divine Reciprocity with the tithe. We give Him ten percent of our gross income and in turn, He gives us insurmountable blessings that we won't have room enough to receive. If we truly put God first in our financial affairs, He will make it possible for us to do more with the remaining ninety percent than we could ever do with one hundred percent. I can personally attest that this is true. It has been found that eight out of ten tithers have zero credit card debt, twenty-eight percent of them are debt free, and thirty-five percent of them have a net worth of $500,000 or more.[xi] I believe that these statistics are a reflection of God's hand on the lives of tithers, providing blessings and giving them wisdom to manage their resources well.

While many people say that they do not have anything to give to others because they have financial needs, the Bible shows us that sowing during famine is wise. In the twenty-sixth chapter of Genesis there was a famine in the land and the Lord told Isaac not to go to Egypt but to stay and dwell in the land of Gerar. God told Isaac that He would bless him and his descendants, giving them the land that He had sworn to give Abraham in an oath.

Isaac heard from God and in obedience, he stayed in the land as God had instructed him. Isaac sowed in that land, and in the same year reaped a hundredfold return, a harvest greater than usual or more than he expected. God abundantly supplied for Isaac and he prospered continually. Isaac was eating when everyone else around him was hungry. From this, we can see that we don't have to be in lack, even when it has been predicted that times will be hard. God will provide—but we must act as well. Isaac did not sit back and cry, "Woe is me." He believed God, sowed and received a great harvest. If we trust God and believe in His Word, He will bless us.

Another example of a person sowing during a time of need is seen in I Kings 17:8-16. Here, the Lord told Elijah to go to Zarephath where God had commanded a widow to provide for Elijah. Elijah went to the woman and asked her for water. As she went to get the water, Elijah asked if she could bring him some bread to eat. The widow told Elijah that she only had a little meal and she was gathering sticks so that she could prepare the last of her provisions for her and her son to eat. Then they would die. Elijah informed the widow that if she made a small cake for him first, God would provide for her and she would have enough for many days.

The widow followed Elijah's instructions and made him a cake to eat first. Afterwards, she prepared for her and her son. Just as Elijah said, the woman's meal did not run out and she was able to provide for her son, herself and Elijah for an extended period.

Many sermons have been preached about sowing in famine and reaping an abundant harvest. However, a key component of these stories is often omitted. In both of these historical accounts of miraculous provision, God initiated the process. He told Isaac to stay in the land, and He would bless him. Isaac obeyed. God had commanded the widow to provide for Elijah, so when Elijah asked her to make the cake for him first, she was not taken by surprise. However, the widow had to get over her fear and exercise two key attributes—faith and obedience.

There are times when there seems to be no way out. It is during these times that sacrificial giving is most advantageous. In 2 Samuel 24:18-24, we see that David had sent his men to count the people of Israel and Judah and in doing so, he sinned against God. In numbering the people, David was indicating that his successes resulted from his valor and the masses of people that he ruled, rather than the power of God. David was giving himself credit when God deserved the praise. We are what we are by the grace of God alone.

Because of his sin, David caused Israel to suffer a penalty. God gave David three choices from which to select his penalty. David chose to fall into the merciful hands of God. Consequently, there was a plague in Israel from which thousands of people died. God instructed Gad, the prophet, to tell David to go to the threshing floor of Araunah and build an altar to the Lord so that the plague would be stopped.

Araunah offered to give David whatever he needed to offer as a sacrifice, but David rejected Araunah's offer. David said that he wanted to buy the threshing floor and the oxen to sacrifice to the Lord because he could not offer that which cost him nothing. David realized that his sin was great, and he was willing to do whatever was necessary to make amends. David sowed a sacrificial offering to God for the purpose of ending the plague. After David offered the burnt offerings, the plague stopped.

Like Isaac and the widow woman, David had heard from God and responded in obedience, sacrificially. Although David gave abundantly, his giving was in response to specific instructions from God. It was God's initiative that caused David to render the sacrificial offering.

People are sowing and expecting God to respond when they have not sought God first, nor do they know His will. Yet, they expect God to give to them as they requested. When they don't receive the requested thing, they feel like giving up all hope. Something is missing in this equation and I assure you that God is not at fault.

Recently, I was approached by a church member who told me that she had sown a lot of seeds in efforts to reap a harvest to meet her needs. She said that she was tired of sowing, and she was going to stop because she had not reaped anything. My heart ached when I heard this and I explained to her that God responds in His timing and she must be patient. Also, she needed to look at her life to see if there were other things that God wanted her to see.

Many people are led to believe that God will work immediately, and they will receive a harvest instantaneously. This is not necessarily true. Galatians 6:7-9 reads as follows: "Do not be deceived, God is not mocked; for whatever a man sows, that he will also reap. For he who sows to his flesh will of the flesh reap corruption, but he who sows to the Spirit will of the Spirit reap everlasting life. And let us not grow weary while doing good, for in due season we shall reap if we do not lose heart" (NKJV). We must wait on the Lord and stay encouraged.

Philippians 4:19 says "And my God shall supply all your need according to His riches in glory by Christ Jesus" (NKJV). Many quote this scripture and really don't know the circumstances around which this scripture is based. The Philippians had given to Paul time and again. When Paul left Macedonia, no other group of Christians gave him as much as the Philippians had given. They also provided Paul's necessities when he was in Thessalonica. Paul told the Philippians that fruit would abound in their account because of what they had done for him. The Philippians would be rewarded because they had given to the needs of the man of God. Therefore, Paul told them that God would supply all their needs according to His riches in glory by Christ Jesus. If we give for the Gospel's sake, God will richly give back to us. We may not receive the harvest immediately, but we can be assured that we will be rewarded. God always provides the best at the most appropriate time, so we must not faint in doing what is right for we will reap benefits. What we give does not compare to the storehouse of God. No bank, stock, bond or investment can out give God.

Prosperity is preached and proclaimed widely and flocks of people are grasping it, attempting to reach the wealthy place full of riches and luxury. If a pastor says that we will be blessed, crowds become ecstatic and some begin to shout and dance in expectation of receiving a blessing. It is true that God wants to bless us, but sadly many will never walk in the abundant life that Jesus proclaimed because they have gotten things out of order in their lives.

Luke 6:38 says: "Give and it will be given to you: good measure, pressed down, shaken together, and running over will be put into your bosom. For with the same measure that you use, it will be measured back to you" (NKJV). We hear this scripture most often during the offering. However, the context from which this verse is taken never mentions money, although it can be applicable. Actually Luke 6:27-38 talks about the rules of kingdom living. In these scriptures, we are told that the kingdom of God has love, forgiveness, no condemnation or judgment, lending and doing for others, asking nothing in return. If we give love, it will be given back to us. If we forgive others, we will be forgiven. The same goes for the other listed attributes that we are to display.

"No one can serve two masters; for either he will hate the one and love the other, or else he will be loyal to the one and despise the other. You cannot serve God and mammon. Therefore I say to you, do not worry about your life, what you will eat or what you will drink; nor about your body, what you will put on. Is not life more than food and the body more than clothing? Look at the birds of the air, for they neither sow nor reap nor gather into barns; yet your heavenly Father feeds them. Are you not of more value than they? Which of you by worrying can add one cubit to his stature? So why do you worry about clothing? Consider the lilies of the field, how they grow; they neither toil nor spin; and yet I say to you that even Solomon in all his glory was not arrayed like one of these. Now if God so clothes the grass of the field, which today is, and tomorrow is thrown into the oven, will He not much more clothe you, O you of little faith? Therefore do not worry, saying 'What shall we eat?' or 'What shall we drink?' or 'What shall we wear?' For after these things the Gentiles seek. For your heavenly Father knows that you need all these things. But seek first the kingdom of God and His righteousness, and all these things shall be added to you" (Matthew 6:24-33, NKJV).

In these scriptures, Jesus clearly tells us not to worry about meeting our needs. He gave examples of how He supplies for birds, flowers and people. I find it interesting that He specifically points out that birds neither sow nor reap nor gather into barns. He was telling us that we don't have to be so focused on having the necessities of life. He would meet our needs. Most importantly, He said that we must seek the kingdom of God and His righteousness first. Everything we need is in the kingdom of God. We don't have to discover ways to make it in this life. Find the kingdom and live righteously, and the other things are privileges of the benefit package afforded to us as citizens of the kingdom.

As Jesus was teaching the disciples to pray, He said that our Father knows what we need before we ask. Because of this, Jesus gave a template of how we should pray in what has become known as "The Lord's Prayer." That prayer states in part: "Our Father which art in heaven, Hallowed be thy name. Thy kingdom come. Thy will be done in earth, as it is in heaven. Give us this day our daily bread. . ." (Matthew 6:9-11, KJV). In this prayer, Jesus was showing us how to approach God, what to request and when to request it. We must always honor and give reverence to God first. God is worthy of all the praise and adoration that we give. Next, we are to ask for the kingdom to come and His will to be done in earth as it is in heaven. With this request, we are asking for people, governments and desires here on earth to be reflective of heaven. We are asking for love, forgiveness, lending, doing good and all the other things that are noted in Luke 6:27-38. The coming of God's kingdom is an assault on the enemy because Satan wants to dominate the earth. We are letting the devil know that his time is limited.

It is only after we acknowledge God, His kingdom, and His will that we should ask for provisions. Most of us pray, seeking our will, not God's will. That's where the controversy begins. I John 5:14,15 says: "Now this is the confidence that we have in Him, that if we ask anything according to His will, He hears us. And if we know that He hears us, whatever we ask, we know that we have the petitions that we have asked of Him" (NKJV). If our will is not the best thing for us, God has no obligation to honor the request. However, if our will and His will are the same, we can be assured that we will obtain whatever we ask.

When we ask for our daily bread (our needs), we are to make the request in faith, confirming that we know God already has provided. We are just waiting for the manifestation or fulfillment of the request. We have been asking for stuff—food, clothing, housing, money and everything our hearts desire, before we seek God and His kingdom. If we are not a part of His kingdom, then we do not have the rights or privileges of citizenship.

Right now, there is a big debate in the United States about a border wall. The President wants to build a wall to keep out those who are attempting illegal entry into our country. Even though some of the people have valid reasons for fleeing their country, they do not have the rights that citizens of the United States have. They are required to have proper documentation in order to enter. They may be good people, but they weren't born here; they do not pay taxes. Therefore, they have no rights or voice in our government. The kingdom of God is based on this same premise. If you are not born again, you lack citizenship of the kingdom.

If we sow without hearing directly from God, knowing His will for a specific situation or having a scriptural basis upon which we are making a request, then there is a great possibility that we will not receive the desired answer to our requests. If you sow for a personal need or request, or if someone asks you to sow for a specific cause, seek God first. He will tell you what to do, whether or not you should give and how much you should give. Sowing for a cause outside of the tithe is a personal choice that comes from the heart (2 Corinthians 9:7).

One of the hardest things about sowing is waiting for the harvest. During this time, our faith is tested and tried. We are tempted to think that God will not answer. It is then that we must use the words of the Bible. Go to the promises and stand on them, knowing that God will respond. We must also not limit God by expecting Him to provide in the way that we think is best. He knows the end from the beginning, so His provision will always be for the greater purpose that He has for us.

Jesus told a parable about sowing seed in Matthew 13:3-8. In this parable, the sower sowed seed on different types of ground. Some seeds fell beside the road, some fell on rocky ground, some fell among thorns and others fell on good soil. Though often used in reference to money, this parable pertains to much more than money. It is referring to sowing the word (message) of the kingdom and its effects on those who hear, receive and respond to it.

Jesus explained the parable saying: "Listen then to the [meaning of the] parable of the sower: While anyone is hearing the Word of the kingdom and does not grasp and comprehend it, the evil one comes and snatches away what was sown in his heart. This is what was sown along the roadside. As for what was sown on thin (rocky) soil, this is he who hears the Word and at once welcomes and accepts it with joy; Yet it has no real root in him, but is temporary (inconstant, lasts but a little while); and when affliction or trouble or persecution comes on account of the Word, at once he is caused to stumble [he is repelled and begins to distrust and desert Him Whom he ought to trust and obey] and he falls away. As for what was sown among thorns, this is he who hears the Word, but the cares of the world and the pleasure and delight and glamour and deceitfulness of riches choke and suffocate the Word, and it yields no fruit. As for what was sown on good soil, this is he who hears the Word and grasps and comprehends it; he indeed bears fruit and yields in one case a hundred times as much as was sown, in another sixty times as much, and in another thirty" (Matthew 13:18-23, AMP).

Those who understand and apply the word of God to their lives and live according to kingdom principles will succeed in everything that they do. "And we know that all things work together for good to those who love God, to those who are the called according to His purpose" (Romans 8:28, NKJV). To the world it will appear as if these people have "the golden touch." In actuality, they have heavenly influence, causing them to produce much more than anyone could imagine. God is able to do "exceedingly and abundantly above all that we ask or think, according to the power that works in us" (Ephesians 3:20).

We talked about the ground in which the Word is sown. There are three major factors that affect your harvest. They are faith, patience and your words. Hebrews 11:6 says "But without faith it is impossible to please Him, for he who comes to God must believe that He is, and that He is a rewarder of those who diligently seek Him" (NKJV). You must believe what God said to you directly, and indirectly, through His Word, the Bible. If you heard God tell you to sow or give and you follow His directive, you will ultimately reap the harvest. If you can find applicable biblical concepts that pertain to your situation, you can expect to reap. I must say that the enemy will tempt you to question the veracity of God's words. Just remember, God's words do not return to Him void. They will accomplish the things that He sent them to do.

One of the hardest things for us to do is wait. Most times, the harvest will not come immediately. God uses time to develop our faith and cause us to trust in Him. While waiting, we must encourage ourselves with the Word. Find scriptures that demonstrate God's nature or His way of doing things. Reflect on how God has provided for you in the past and by all means, concentrate on the positive. Only say those things that are in alignment with the Word of God and refuse to listen to contrary opinions.

Many times, instead of waiting patiently for God to respond, we think we need to "help" Him. I am reminded of the first time I cooked rice when I was a child. I put the rice in the pot, along with the water, salt and butter, and let it boil. After stirring, I placed the lid on the pot and reduced the heat to simmer. All I needed to do was let the rice continue to cook for fifteen minutes and it would have been done. Unfortunately, I kept looking in the pot, stirring the rice and expecting it to cook properly. After stirring several times within fifteen minutes, I turned the stove off. The result was a gooey mess that no one could eat. My brother looked at the rice and just laughed at me. He fell on the floor, and asked how I expected him to be able to go to work with his chest stuck together. Older brothers can really make the younger siblings know how badly they miss the mark. I was so hurt that I cried profusely. My dad came to my rescue, told me it was alright, and that he appreciated me trying to cook. He attempted to eat a little, just to make me feel better. My impatience and eagerness to cook the rice faster created something inedible. Even I wouldn't eat that rice.

Because of my impatience and unnecessary stirring, I made things worse. We, in like manner, do the same when we interfere, trying to make God work in our timing. We intercede and "fix" things only to make them worse and increase the time we have to wait. But, God acts just as my dad did toward me. He comforts us and gently guides us to the right path, showing us that He knows best.

We reap a harvest in many ways. We reap what we sow, in proportion to what we sow, more than what we sow and from what others have sown. For example, if you are kind to others, you will receive kindness in return. If you give a lot, you will receive a lot in return. As in the case of the tithe, you will have blessings that are more than you can receive. If you walk in God's chosen purpose for your life, you will in turn be more productive than you could ever be in any other walk of life. You will also be happier doing the work of your calling. Lastly, all of us have reaped what others have sown. The sacrifices of our forefathers, parents and most of all Jesus Christ have given us opportunities and blessings, for which we are eternally grateful.

Chapter 7 – Things to Ponder

1. Do you believe that the principle of sowing and reaping applies to every aspect of life? Why or why not?

   _____
   _____
   _____
   _____
   _____

2. When and how should we sow?

   _____
   _____
   _____
   _____
   _____

3. Is where we sow important? How does The Parable of the Sower explain this?

   _____
   _____
   _____
   _____
   _____

4. What are three major factors that affect your harvest?

5. Read Matthew 6:33. Why is it important to seek the Kingdom of God first?

6. How does following kingdom principles affect your level of success?

CHAPTER 8

Displaced Trust

> "I remember saying to my mentor, 'If I had more money, I would have a better plan.' He quickly responded, 'I would suggest that if you had a better plan, you would have more money.' You see, it's not the amount that counts; it's the plan that counts."
> – Jim Rohn

Everybody is trying to get ahead, to make it to the top and stay there. Consequently, we often listen to the world and follow their suggestions about success. In Matthew 6:33, 34, we are told to seek first the kingdom of God and His righteousness and all the other things that we need would be given to us by God. Somehow, we have gotten this principle confused, thinking that we are our own suppliers. Deuteronomy 8:18 says: "And you shall remember the Lord your God, for it is He who gives you power to get wealth that He may establish His covenant which He swore to your fathers, as it is this day" (NKJV). We must remember that everything we have is a result of God's mercy and grace. Unfortunately, there are those who do not know or understand this basic truth. The world teaches that only the strong survive and that survival is among the fittest. The richest and fastest also think that they are the reason for their own successes. These things make us think that the ability to cope with life and attain levels of success are solely dependent upon us—our work, achievements, money and tenacity. **We acquire wealth only through the grace and power of God.**

"Then He spoke a parable to them, saying 'The ground of a certain rich man yielded plentifully. And he thought within himself, saying, 'What shall I do, since I have no room to store my crops?' So he said, 'I will do this: I will pull down my barns and build greater, and there I will store all my crops and my goods. And I will say to my soul, Soul, you have many goods laid up for many years; take your ease; eat, drink and be merry.' But God said to him, 'Fool! This night your soul will be required of you; then whose will those things be which you have provided?' So is he who lays up treasure for himself, and is not rich toward God" (Luke 12:16-21, NKJV). In these verses, we read about the rich man who did not regard or handle his wealth as God requires. The man had great wealth and viewed himself as the source of his riches. Then, he failed to think about God or anyone else other than himself. He continued to look at what he had and created means to store his wealth so that he could live lavishly. God says that doing this is foolish. We cannot truly have an abundant life without God in the center. The rich man was not saving and setting aside for the future as a wise steward. He was trusting in his own ability and abundance rather than trusting in God. God wants us to put material and financial wealth in their proper place.

We have talked about saving and investing, and being a good steward over the things that have been given to us. While it is wise to save and invest, we must not make them the focus of our existence, becoming our god. I know people who work extensive hours, ignoring their families, in order to increase their savings. They work so much that they miss important family events and milestones in their children's lives. Their marriages fall apart and they lose touch with everybody and everything except money. While God wants us to save and be wise stewards, he does not want us to make money a god, forsaking life, family and even our health to acquire more of it. We must keep money in its proper perspective, using it to live but not living to get it. If we put God first, He promises to take care of us. We don't have to worry.

It takes a lot of energy to worry. We lose sleep, destroying our health, relationships and our future by worrying needlessly. It has been found that most of the things that we worry about never happen, yet we continue to waste time and energy on this exercise in futility. We are to be anxious for nothing and give everything to God when we pray. When we truly trust God, we will have peace and our needs will be met as well. In fact, God will meet and exceed our needs if we have faith to believe.

Not too long ago, I had to make a big financial decision. I wrestled with the choices that were before me and I prayed for God's direction. I quoted scriptures and reminded God that the Word says in James 1:5 to ask God when we lack wisdom, and He would give it to us liberally. I waited and waited, looking for God to explicitly tell me which choice to make. I wondered why He didn't just come out and direct me to take option A or option B. I heard absolutely nothing, or so I thought.

One thing you will learn as you grow in Christ is that God does not complete a puzzle all at once. He gives us one piece at a time. One night, I was sitting on my loveseat and I felt the presence of God so strongly. Then He said two words: "Trust Me." I knew beyond a shadow of a doubt that I had heard God, but had no idea what I was supposed to do. I kept looking and asking until I finally realized that God wanted me to understand that He was with me and that He had provided the resources for me to make the right decision with His help. He was not going to let me fall as long as I acknowledged Him as the head of my life, not my resources. I was learning to live out the words of Proverbs 3:5, 6, which says, "Trust in the Lord with all your heart, and lean not on your own understanding. In all your ways acknowledge Him, and He shall direct your paths" (NKJV). I made my decision and found that the choice I selected was more advantageous than I had thought; I was going to be just fine. God wanted me to grow up, trust Him, and take a step in faith, knowing that His outreached hand is there to hold and stabilize me to keep me from falling. Sometimes growing up is not easy, but in the long run, we will see that everything God allows us to go through is being used to ultimately work for our good.

Sometimes people are like I was, waiting, praying and believing that God is going to come down and just take over whatever situation they are in and fix it. He doesn't work like that. He wants us to exercise our faith, because faith without works is dead. Hebrews 11:6 says "But without faith it is impossible to please Him, for he who comes to God must believe that He is, and that He is a rewarder of those who diligently seek Him" (NKJV). We must move out of God's way and allow Him to move us up.

The need for and acquisition of money can control us and become the center of our lives, if we let it. The Bible advises us against this. "Do not lay up for yourselves treasures on earth, where moth and rust destroy and where thieves break in and steal; but lay up for yourselves treasures in heaven, where neither moth nor rust destroys and where thieves do not break in and steal. For where your treasure is, there your heart will be also" (Matthew 6:19-21, NKJV). If we treasure money, our resources or abilities, we in essence give those things our heart. If we love things with all of our heart, then we cannot and will not love, trust and serve God as we should. We cannot serve God and mammon. We must choose who or what will be the head of our lives.

Chapter 8 – Things to Ponder

1. How does the way you handle your money demonstrate your trust in God?

   _____

   _____

   _____

   _____

   _____

2. What does "where your treasure is, there will your heart be also" mean?

   _____

   _____

   _____

   _____

   _____

3. How does God speak to you? How do you know His voice?

   _____

   _____

   _____

   _____

   _____

4. What happens when you only think about yourself and your needs?

   _____
   _____
   _____
   _____
   _____

CHAPTER 9

Decision Time

> "We are accountable for our actions as we exercise our moral agency. If we understand this principle and make righteous choices, our lives will be blessed."
> – L. Lionel Kendrick

After reading the previous chapters, you may be ready to make some changes in your life. If you aren't a tither and you feel God speaking to you about the tithe, then I encourage you to begin to give ten percent of your gross income and see how God will bless you. When you list your bills, place the tithe at the top, giving first place to God. Making the tithe a priority demonstrates your commitment to God. He will reciprocate, just as He promised.

In the fourth chapter of Genesis, we read about Cain and Abel. Cain presented an offering to God whenever he felt like it, but this dishonored God. Abel brought the firstborn of his flock. God respected Abel and his offering, but He did not accept Cain's. In the same way, God will see if we really honor and trust Him by the way we give. We should be eager to bring the tithe to church and place it in the basket with thanksgiving. Remember, Jesus receives our tithes.

Perhaps there is no extra money in your household. You may think it is too difficult for you to tithe. Tithing is not based upon how much is left over. It is given first. Remember that tithing is a percentage of your income, not a set dollar amount. The dollar amount may be large or small, depending upon your income, but the impact is proportionately the same for everyone. If you only have one dollar, give God ten cents, and He will bless you abundantly for that act of faith and obedience. God said to prove Him, and He would open the windows of heaven and pour out a blessing that you would not have room enough to receive. Try Him.

Maybe, you just don't have enough faith to step out. You don't have to be like I was. I didn't know the word of God like I do now when I began tithing. And at that time we were not in a church that taught the Word as my pastor does in my church today. In that case, you need a plan. Go to your Bible and write the scriptures concerning the promises of God and learn them. You can even use internet search engines to learn more about biblical topics and find the scriptures easily. Meditate on the scriptures and repeat them to yourself throughout each day so that the Word of God becomes embedded in your innermost being. When praying, remind God of what He said. He cannot let His Word return to Him void, so He will fulfill all of His promises. As you build your faith, having full confidence in God, you will be able to tithe easily.

Once you make the decision to tithe, you must understand that the enemy will throw darts and attack you in any way he can. When this happens, stand and be determined to see God work. Ephesians 6:12 says, "We aren't fighting against human enemies but against rulers, authorities, forces of cosmic darkness, and spiritual powers of evil in the heavens" (CEB). God is more powerful than Satan and his imps. They are using a scare tactic. The enemy will put all kinds of negative thoughts in your mind. Reject those thoughts and think about a positive outcome. You must trust God. He will come to your rescue in ways that will amaze you. Don't put God in a box, trying to get Him to provide the financial resources the way you think He should do it. You and I do not have the capacity to fully understand how much God can and will do when we trust Him. Let go and let God do what only He can do.

If you are expecting God to rain thousands of dollars from heaven, it won't come out of the sky, or magically appear on your doorstep, but He will work on your behalf. Doors of opportunity can open. Debts can be canceled. Ideas can be generated, wisdom can be provided, and so much more. The possibilities are endless when it comes to God. Wait in expectancy and be ready to receive.

Recently, I had an unexpected cancellation of a debt. I had gone to the endodontist to have a root canal. After the procedure was over, I went to the receptionist to pay my bill and she informed me that the doctor was not charging me the coinsurance for which I was responsible. That was an unexpected blessing from God, which saved me hundreds of dollars. I thanked God and the doctor. We never know how God will work on our behalf. I hadn't prayed about the cost, or asked God to intervene. He blessed me, just because He is God.

Sometimes, people already have sufficient resources, but they need to learn how to manage what they have. The Parable of the Talents lets us know that God expects us to use or manage our resources wisely. You must be faithful over a few things before you will be given the opportunity to rule over much more.

My husband and I tithed for many years and still struggled because we did not properly manage what we had. Like many people, we had a lot of stuff that we really didn't need. After getting tired of living from paycheck to paycheck, we made a decision to change the way we lived. As promotions and increases in income came, we paid more on debts to pay them off and began to save more. To do that we had to make choices. We had to make a conscious decision to stop spending needlessly. We had to establish a budget and follow it.

Getting out of debt will not happen overnight. It is a process. Yes, God can work miracles, but His ultimate goal is for us to be mature in Him. My husband and I had to learn how to handle and manage what we had so that we could be trusted with more. We cannot have and may not need everything that the Joneses have. God will bless us and we can get more, as we learn how to establish a good relationship with money. We cannot love money or things. We must seek God's way of doing things and His righteousness first. Then God, the owner of all, will abundantly supply everything we need; He will also give us many of our wants. It is all in perspective and proper handling of what has been given to us.

Getting out of debt requires a plan. We must know where we want to go before we start the journey. First decide what you want to accomplish, then set out to do it. Proverbs 29:18 says "Where there is no vision, the people perish: but he that keepeth the law, happy is he" (KJV). Also, you must follow the advice given in Habakkuk 2:2 and write the vision, identifying your goals and objectives so that they can be clearly followed. In the corporate environment, we had to write goals for ourselves and our employees each year. The goals were to be S.M.A.R.T. goals, which had to be:

S pecific
M easurable
A ttainable
R eliable
T ime Driven

In essence, we had to list goals that indicated what we wanted to do, how we wanted to do it, and when we wanted to reach those markers. Use this same mindset when set, your financial goals. Be specific and list ways that you c. measure your progress in time increments. Most importantly, make them attainable. It would not make sense to set a goal of becoming a millionaire in two years if you have no money, resources or job today. Barring a miracle from God, you probably won't reach that goal. When setting your financial objectives, use S.M.A.R.T. goals, knowing that it is a process that will take time and effort. Leave room to reward yourself and don't become defeated if immediate success is not seen. It will come, if you do not give up.

To get out of debt, first you must know where you are. Write down your income and expenses. List everything you spend money on, even the little things like breakfast at a fast food restaurant. It's the little foxes that destroy the vine. It's the nickels and dimes, dollar here and dollar there that really add up. You may need to track your outgoing funds over a period of time, like for two weeks or a month for example, in order to get a true picture of how you spend your money. I suggest tracking expenditures for two week periods because many of you are paid every two weeks. Monitor yourself from paycheck to paycheck or monthly. This will require time and discipline, but it is necessary so that you can get a true picture of your current financial position.

If you are experiencing a financial crisis, possibly resulting from the loss of a job, sickness or death of a loved one, many banks and credit card companies offer options to adjust your payment. Also, there are hospitals that completely forgive debts that are owed to them. Call your creditors and explain your situation. You may be able to make adjustments that will not affect your credit, or they may forgive your debt. However, if they provide new payment options, you must live up to your promises. If you ask for an extension to pay a bill by a specific date, then you must do it. If you have extenuating circumstances that affect your ability to fulfill your promise, then call the creditor. Don't ignore your obligations because they will not automatically disappear. Be a man or woman of honor, living up to your commitments.

If you are strapped for cash, you may even want to sell some of your property or have a yard sale. Bartering is another way that people earn extra money. You may offer to provide a service to others in exchange for a service that you need. This creates a win/win situation for both of you. If you are unemployed or under employed, another job or part-time employment may be needed.

A prime time to sow is when you are in need. Giving as God directs you in these times exemplifies your dependence upon Him and expectation of deliverance from Him. (This does not replace the tithe). The widow of Zarephath in I Kings 17:7-16 was gathering sticks to make the final meal for her and her son. Elijah told her to make a small cake for him first, and then make something for herself and her son. Elijah encouraged the widow by telling her that the Lord said that her flour and oil would not run out until the day that it rained. The widow gave a cake to Elijah first and sure enough, the widow's and her son's needs were met as Elijah prophesied. Sowing as God directs you is always beneficial.

There are lots of financial planning tools that you can retrieve from the internet. Or, you can simply enter your information on a spreadsheet like I did. The goal is to get an accurate assessment of your financial situation. Once you complete your financial analysis, look for ways that you can save money and reduce your expenses. There are things that most of us spend money on without thinking about it, like going through the drive-thru window or ordering a pizza. These add up quickly and when compiled can be used as additional money to pay on bills.

You always want to pay more than the minimum on credit cards. Creditors set the payments so that they can make as much money from you as possible. The borrower is the servant to the lender and you will be enslaved to creditors for decades if you don't pay more than the minimum amount. The two most suggested methods of paying off credit cards is to 1) pay off the card with the highest interest first or 2) pay off the card with the lowest balance first. Though paying off the balance with the highest interest will save more money, either of these methods works to your advantage. My husband and I paid off the card with the lowest balance first. After paying off each card, we added the amount of money that had been paid on the previous card(s) to the payment on the next card and accelerated that payoff. By paying off the smallest amount first, we were able to experience a level of success sooner and stay motivated to continue. There is great joy when you get a bill with a zero balance.

There are three common methods of consolidating debts that I would like to discuss: transferring all credit card balances to another card, obtaining a consolidation loan from a bank and seeking the services of a debt consolidation company. Let's discuss each separately.

Transferring all credit card balances may be a viable option for paying off debt if the card has an interest rate that is lower than what you currently have. However, beware of introductory offers that have a variable rate that increases after a set period. When the interest rate increases on these accounts, you could end up paying more per month than you paid initially on the separate accounts. If this happens you will not only pay more, but it may even take you longer to pay off the debt.

When using a bank or a debt consolidating company as a means of lowering your monthly payments, it is wise to look at more than the amount of your monthly payment. Consider the interest rate and the length of time that it will take you to pay off the loan. Just because you may have a lower monthly payment, you may not be saving money if it takes you longer to pay it off. Also, there are some unscrupulous debt consolidating companies that are anxious to lend anyone money. These companies tack on enormous fees to your debt and stretch payments out for years at ridiculously high interest rates. Those with low credit scores are prime targets for these companies.

Once you get out of credit card debt, and finish paying car loans, school loans, or other loans, then mortgage payoff should be the final goal. Look for lower interest rates and refinance only if you can quickly recover the costs and fees associated with refinancing and if you intend to stay in your home for an extended period of time. If all of your other bills are paid off, then you could make just as much progress by making mortgage payments every two weeks, or by adding additional principle to your monthly payment. Both of these methods pare down interest and accelerate the mortgage payoff. If you receive a tax refund, consider using some or all of the refund to pay toward your mortgage principle. You will be surprised at how much of an impact this makes.

"Budget" is often considered a dirty word because it brings negative emotions and unhappiness. Living on a budget is like being on a financial diet. We hate the process, but we sure like to dress up the new body when we reach the finish line. Start by listing your income, including funds from every source that you receive each month. Then list your expenses, breaking them down into categories like housing, utilities, transportation, loans, credit cards, et cetera. As with any diet, your financial plan must leave room for some enjoyment and freedom. Don't forget to factor in time for fun, entertainment and some of the niceties that you enjoy. However, vacations and expensive trips should be delayed until debts are reduced and/or eliminated. Moderation is required until you reach your final goal. Just a note: this will take some time and will not be an overnight process. I assure you, it is well worth the effort. Once you get out of debt, don't revert to old spending habits.

Seeking God first, obeying His word and following His plan and principles will lead you to the financial success that God has ordained for you since the beginning of time. It is yours. Go out and get it.

Chapter 9 – Things to Ponder

1. If you are not a tither, state why you think it does not apply to you.

   _____

   _____

   _____

   _____   _____

   _____

2. What are ways that you can build your faith to tithe?

   _____

   _____

   _____

   _____

   _____

3. What are some of the ways that the windows of heaven will open to pour out blessings?

   _____

   _____

   _____

   _____

   _____

4. Are you managing your resources well? If not, what can you do to improve?

_____
_____
_____
_____
_____

5. What are S.M.A.R.T. goals?

_____
_____
_____
_____

6. Do you have a financial plan? If not, develop one, start by setting goals now.

_____
_____
_____
_____
_____

CHAPTER 10

Stepping into the Future

> "The only limit to our realization of tomorrow will be our doubts of today. Let us move forward with strong and active faith."
> – Franklin D. Roosevelt

When I left my job, I had no idea what I would do with my future. I only knew that I had a passion for helping others learn and understand the promises of God. I had a dream, a desire and no real plan of action. I had finished teaching a series of Sunday school classes, and I was preparing for new classes to submit to our pastor for approval. I had no idea that this book would evolve. I had been working on another project and thought it was supposed to be the makings of a book. I guess that will be next.

I began to spend more time in the presence God, praying, reading and asking for direction. When asked for specifics about His plans for me, I only felt Him say in my spirit that He would show me piece by piece. I had to walk by faith and not by sight. I would take a step, pray and ask God for the next step, which many times had to be taken in faith as well. Along the way, there were words of encouragement, prophecies and confirmations from God that He was guiding me.

Even though I had not planned to stop working when I did, the peace of God kept me. I became more confident that I had done the right thing because I enjoyed working on things that mattered for the kingdom of God. I was learning that seeking God first really is the best thing to do for my peace and my future. I must mention, especially since this book pertains to God's financial plan, that I had resources available to meet my financial needs when I stopped working and I continued to give my tithes. I did not miss any meals, though I probably could have gone without eating with no ill effect.

The most important fact in all of this is that God opened a door of opportunity for me that I never anticipated. During classes that I taught, I saw the need for in-depth teaching on God's financial principles. I did not know that the pastor had already spoken to two elders about the commencement of classes on this topic. I was asked to join the team. As a result, I began to write this book.

In our financial management classes, we discuss not only God's financial principles, but also simple steps each of us can take to reach financial freedom. People are learning that they are not alone and that while their challenges may appear to be overwhelming, they can be conquered. Through the word of God and encouragement, lives are changing.

Some of you may be thinking that it is too late for you to find your purpose. I am a witness that it is never too late. God can redeem the time and make you more successful in you latter years than you ever were. God has equipped all of us with gifts that await the prime time for the revelation of their divine purpose. As you walk closer to Him, life will be more fulfilling. He will unveil things for you just as He did for me. You will have rivers, streams, brooks, lakes, springs and wells that will flow with financial blessings that only God can provide when you follow Him in faith and obedience.

I trust that you have been inspired to truly seek the kingdom of God and His righteousness before anything else. I assure you that you will be better for it and you will lack nothing.

Chapter 10 – Points to Ponder

1. Do you know what your purpose or gift is? Are you walking in that purpose and/or using your gift?

   _____
   _____
   _____
   _____
   _____

2. How can you find your God-given purpose or gift?

   _____
   _____
   _____
   _____
   _____

3. Why would your life be more fulfilling after you find your purpose or gift?

   _____
   _____
   _____
   _____
   _____

4. Why would you have financial success when you find your purpose or gift?

_____
_____
_____
_____
_____

Endnotes

[i] James Strong, LL.D., S.T.D., *The New Strong's Exhaustive Concordance of the Bible,* Tennessee, Thomas Nelson Publishers, 1990, # 6030.

[ii] *This is the Number-One Cause of Stress for Americans,* November 1, 2017 (accessed April 8, 2018); available from http://time.com/5005076/stress-anxiety-symptoms/

[iii] Larry Kreider, *God's Perspective on Finances*, Updated Edition ©2002, (Ephrata: House to House Publications), 8.

[iv] *7 Startling Facts: An Up Close Look at Church Attendance in America*, April 18, 2018 (accessed May 21, 2018) available from https://churchleaders.com/pastors/pastor-articles/139575-7-startling-facts-an-up-close-look-at-church-attendance-in-america.html/

[v] James Strong, LL.D., S.T.D., *The New Strong's Exhaustive Concordance of the Bible*, #3533.

[vi] Ibid, #7287.

[vii] *Life Insurance Industry Under Investigation*, April 17, 2016 (accessed February 2, 2019), available from https://www.cbsnews.com/news/60-minutes-life-insurance-investigation-lesley-stahl/

[viii] *21 Fascinating Tithing Statistics*, October 5, 2014 (accessed May 22, 2018), available from https://healthresearchfunding.org/21-tithing-statistics/

[ix] Ibid.

[x] Ibid.

[xi] Ibid.

Bibliography

7 Startling Facts: An Up Close Look at Church Attendance in America, April 10, 2018 (accessed May 21, 2018) available from https://churchleaders.com/pastors/pastor-articles/139575-7-startling-facts-an-up-close-look-at-church-attendance-in-america.html/.

Health Research Funding Organization, *21 Fascinating Tithing Statistics*, October 5, 2014 (accessed May 22, 2018), available from https://healthresearchfunding.org/21-tithing-statistics.

Kreider, Larry. *God's Perspective on Finances*. Updated Edition. Lititz. House to House Publications, 2002.

Moore, Michael D. *God's Heavenly Banking System*. Birmingham: Faith Chapel Christian Center, 2000.

Stahl, Lesley, *Life Insurance Industry Under Investigation*, April 17, 2016 (accessed February 2, 2019), available from https://www.cbsnews.com/news/60-minutes-life-insurance-investigation-lesley-stahl/

Strong, James, LL.D, S.T.D. *The New Strong's Exhaustive Concordance of the Bible* .Nashville: Thomas Nelson, Inc., 1990.

This is the Number-One Cause of Stress for Americans. November 1, 2017. Available from http://time.com/5005076/stress-anxiety-symptoms/.

Contact information

Deborah Alexander
c/o God's Mighty Dollar
P.O. Box 241164
Little Rock, Arkansas 72223

Godsmightydollar@gmail.com